HEALTH AND FITNESS

IN FOCUS

CONTENTS

This edition published 1991 by
Franklin Watts
96 Leonard Street
London EC2A 4RH

ISBN 0 7496 0505 7

Printed in Belgium

Original edition published 1990 by
Hobsons Publishing plc
Produced in conjunction with and sponsored by The Health Promotion Research Trust

A CIP catalogue record for this book is available from the British Library

Consultant editors: Dr W Mason
Dr Michael Reiss
Editor: Dr Kathryn Leighton

The Health Promotion Research Trust encourages people to adopt a more responsible attitude to their health. For a complete list of publications, please write to:

The Health Promotion Trust
49-53 Regent Street
Cambridge CB2 1AB

Acknowledgements
We are grateful to the following for supplying photographic material: All Sport, Cement Association, General Dental Council, Health Education Authority, Health Promotion Research Trust, Ralph Hutchings, Images Colour Library, Nike, Pasta Information Service, Phoenix/Jess Stock, Queen's University of Belfast/Craig Mahoney, Roche, Science Photo Library, Scottish Sports Council, Sea Fish Industry Authority, Mark Shearman, Tony Stone Worldwide, Zoe Whishaw.

Specific findings by the following scientists who have received funding from the Health Promotion Research Trust are among the work described in the text: Dr. M. Blaxter (University of Cambridge), Dr. M. Burr (MRC Epidemiology Unit, Cardiff), Dr. P. Cooper (University of Cambridge), Dr. B. Cox (University of Cambridge), Professor C. George (University of Southampton), Professor K. Laurence (University of Wales College of Medicine), Mr. A. Nichols (The Queen's University of Belfast), Professor A. Steptoe (St. George's Hospital Medical School), Dr. W. Tancred (University of Sheffield), Dr. B. Tew (University of Wales College of Medicine), Dr. J. Wardle (Institute of Psychiatry, University of London) and Ms. M. Whichelow (University of Cambridge.)

HEALTH AND FITNESS

IN FOCUS

Hilary Tunnicliffe

FRANKLIN WATTS
LONDON • NEW YORK • SYDNEY • TORONTO

1: WHAT IS HEALTH?

The World Health Organization defines health as 'a state of complete economic, physical, mental and social well-being'. In other words, to be healthy it is not enough just to be physically fit and well, you must feel good about the way you are and be satisfied with your way of life. These four components of health are very closely linked.

WHY BE HEALTHY?
Being healthy is about feeling good, being as fit as you can and living a full and contented life. There will be times when you are not in the best of health, and this book is to help you to recognise when this happens, and give you some ideas about what to do to improve your health.

HOW TO BE HEALTHY
There is no one formula for being healthy. What it is to be healthy varies according to the kind of person you are, and also what age you are. You cannot be expected to take responsibility for your health if you have no idea what this entails.

The best way of ensuring the good health of a population is to try to keep people healthy, by educating them to look after themselves, and to prevent as many illnesses as possible. Curing diseases and mending broken bodies should be seen as the last strategy rather than the first. The National Health Service exists in our country to try to ensure that the general population enjoys good health, but most of its resources are still spent in treating ill health.

One important step to achieving health is health education for which the Health Education Authority has overall responsibility. General practitioners, health visitors, health education units and schools help by teaching us what good health is, and how to look after ourselves. Voluntary organizations like charities, helplines and charitable trusts such as The Health Promotion Research Trust also help to get health messages across to the public. Because there are many sides to health, it is important that research is carried out into the factors affecting our health and how to counteract those causing ill health. One example of this is the effects of cigarette smoking on health. Up to about thirty years ago, it was not realised quite how harmful cigarette smoking is. It is now described as the 'single most avoidable risk to our health'. Education informs us of these risks so that we can avoid things which might be harmful to our health.

The most important step to health is to avoid illness. One way of ensuring protection against some diseases and disorders is preventive medicine. Immunisation programmes can stop us falling ill and prevent epidemics of certain diseases. Globally, the disease smallpox has been eradicated by a worldwide vaccination programme.

Age	Vaccine	Details
3–6 months	Triple vaccine (DPT)	Primary course which protects against diphtheria, whooping cough (pertussis) and tetanus. Polio vaccine given by mouth at the same time.
4–6 weeks later	Second triple vaccine	
6–9 months after second vaccine	Third triple vaccine	
15 months (or 1 month after successful completion of Primary course)	Measles, mumps and rubella	
4–5 years (or 3 years after successful completion of Primary course)	Diphtheria, tetanus and polio boosters	
10–13 years	BCG	Protects against tuberculosis.Only given if skin test shows no natural immunity.
13 years (girls only)	Rubella/German measles	Protects against German measles as the virus can harm the developing baby if disease is contracted during pregnancy.
15 years	Tetanus and polio booster	

A timetable of the vaccinations necessary to prevent serious infections such as poliomyelitis (polio) or tuberculosis (TB).

By taking responsibility for our own health and by helping our families to learn about health and fitness we can help to ensure that people of all age groups enjoy good health.

HOW MUCH OF OUR HEALTH IS UNDER OUR CONTROL?

We are all born different. Our physical characteristics are inherited, and so, by the time we are born, characteristics like our sex, our potential height and our eye colour are already decided. We cannot change any of these things naturally.

Some people are born disabled. They may be mentally handicapped or physically handicapped. They may have an inherited disease, such as cystic fibrosis, which puts some restrictions on their way of life.

Mental handicaps include Down's syndrome and brain damage due to illness, injury or problems during birth. Physical handicaps include cerebral palsy, blindness, deafness, spina bifida (where the spinal cord doesn't develop properly) and physical deformities where your body may be born different from others.

HEALTH AND THE DISABLED

Disabilities can mean that you are unable to lead exactly the same kind of life as other people. This does not mean that you can't be healthy. It would be unrealistic to compare your level of physical fitness with a super-fit athlete, but that doesn't mean that you are unfit and therefore unhealthy. Being healthy is about being as fit, contented and happy as you can be within your own particular circumstances.

Many people spend hours wishing they were different but most physical characteristics are fixed long before birth and cannot be changed significantly. It is better to make the most of your good points rather than dwelling on those you don't like.

Many sports can be enjoyed by physically and mentally handicapped people. Games like basketball can be played from wheelchairs to a very high level. The participants are extremely fit, and play in specially adapted wheelchairs. Many sports are available for the handicapped, either by using specially adapted apparatus and equipment or by slightly modifying the playing rules. If you are physically handicapped, you often develop other muscle groups or senses to a very high level to compensate for your disability.

Physical or mental handicap need not be a barrier that prevents people from enjoying sport.

SPINA BIFIDA; A CASE STUDY

Research workers at the University of Wales have studied young adults who are handicapped with spina bifida. It was found that most of their health problems were not connected with their disability.

The young people were asked for their views on the help they had received with their schooling, training and occupational and social integration, and were also asked how much help they were still getting. It turned out that the achievements of spina bifidas at school were linked to their academic abilities: some reached HND and degree standard. The richness of their social lives depended on their characters and where they lived. Those who were less severely handicapped and had outgoing personalities enjoyed the fullest lives.

Other important factors of physical health are watching what you eat, and avoiding unhealthy habits like smoking, drinking too much alcohol or taking unprescribed drugs and medicines.

When medicines are prescribed, it is helpful to know about their effects before you take them. In experiments piloted in Hampshire, information leaflets were distributed with medicines by pharmacists.

Patients who had read the pamphlets followed the instructions better than people who had just been told what to do, and were more aware that they should store their medicines carefully and get rid of any left over. They were also more satisfied with their treatment.

Some aspects of physical health are, therefore, under our control. We can all work to ensure that we are as physically healthy as possible, and follow any treatment properly.

Another aspect of health is mental health. As this depends on pressures from outside as well as our attitudes and emotions, it is difficult to say how much is under our control. Part of trying to be healthy is about understanding ourselves and recognising when we need a change.

A feeling of social well-being means that you are happy with your lifestyle – the way you live and the conditions in which you find yourself. This involves not only your well-being, but that of your family and friends. Again, you may only be able to control parts of this, as you are dealing with others who may have different ideas from you and also who may still have responsibility for you.

Living a healthy life will not prevent us from getting old. No one can live for ever, although, with healthy living, we may be able to live longer and improve the quality of our lives, especially in old age.

It would be difficult to be healthy in this environment.

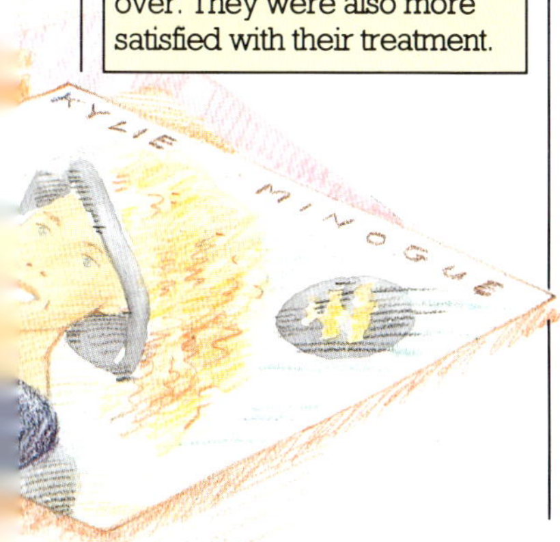

June

MONDAY **9**

Went to school
Got into trouble for not doing my
homework. Mr Smith is going to
write home. Mum'll go nuts. I don't
want to go home. Hamburger and
chips for lunch again. My spots!
Games this afternoon. Won volley-
ball game. Brilliant! Had a fag on
the bus going home. Didn't like it,
but you get laughed at if you
don't join in. Maybe I should bike
in tomorrow so I don't have to
sit with the smokers.
Watched TV this evening. Boring

What do you think of this person? Is he in a healthy state?
Write down the good things about his day, and the bad things.

2: HEALTHY EATING

In order to be physically healthy, we need to eat a balanced diet. Balanced diets contain the right amounts of seven food groups. We use the food we eat to produce fuel to give energy, for building materials so that we grow and repair ourselves and for maintaining a constant environment for our bodies. Malnutrition, or bad eating, can lead to serious health problems. We need to balance the amount we eat so that we have enough energy, but not too much, as we store the excess as fat and that can also lead to problems.

A BALANCED DIET
A balanced diet consists of carbohydrate, protein, fat, vitamins, minerals, fibre and water. If you eat a varied diet of fresh food, it is likely that you will be getting a good balance of these food groups. You do not need them in equal amounts. Protein, fibre, carbohydrates and fats are needed in relatively large proportions, whereas small amounts of many different vitamins and minerals are required. It is rare to find a food which is, for example, pure protein or pure carbohydrate. Most foods contain a mixture of different groups.

In a survey of over 9000 adults in the UK, knowledge of which foods contain dietary fibre was tested. Women were significantly more knowledgeable than men except about white bread.

Food	Fibre-rich?	% men correct	% women correct
Wheat flakes	Yes	92	95
Eggs	No	79	78
Apples	Yes	46	53
Cheese	No	75	74
Orange juice	No	68	65
White bread	Yes	46	38
Potatoes	Yes	41	51
Roast beef	No	51	51

Notice that all the foods which are rich in fibre are of plant origin (the juice of the orange is fibre-free, and the fibre is in the pulp, which is of course left in the squeezer). Notice, also, that about half the group were wrong in some of their replies.

Maltose, a disaccharide

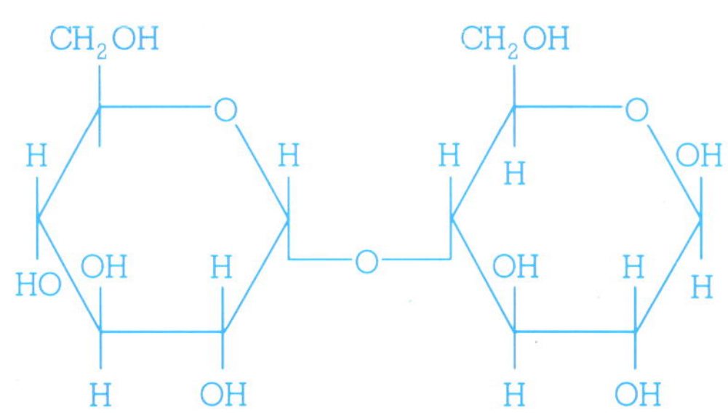

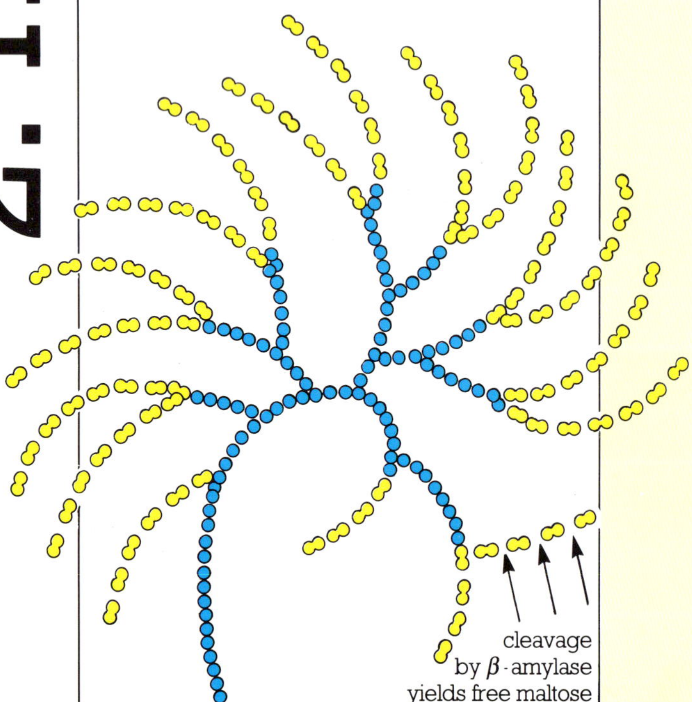

Amylopectin, a polysaccharide

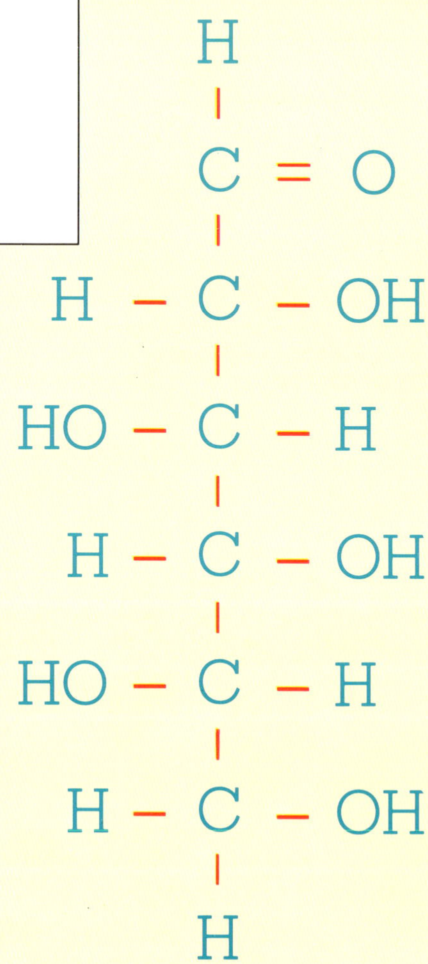

Glucose, a monosaccharide

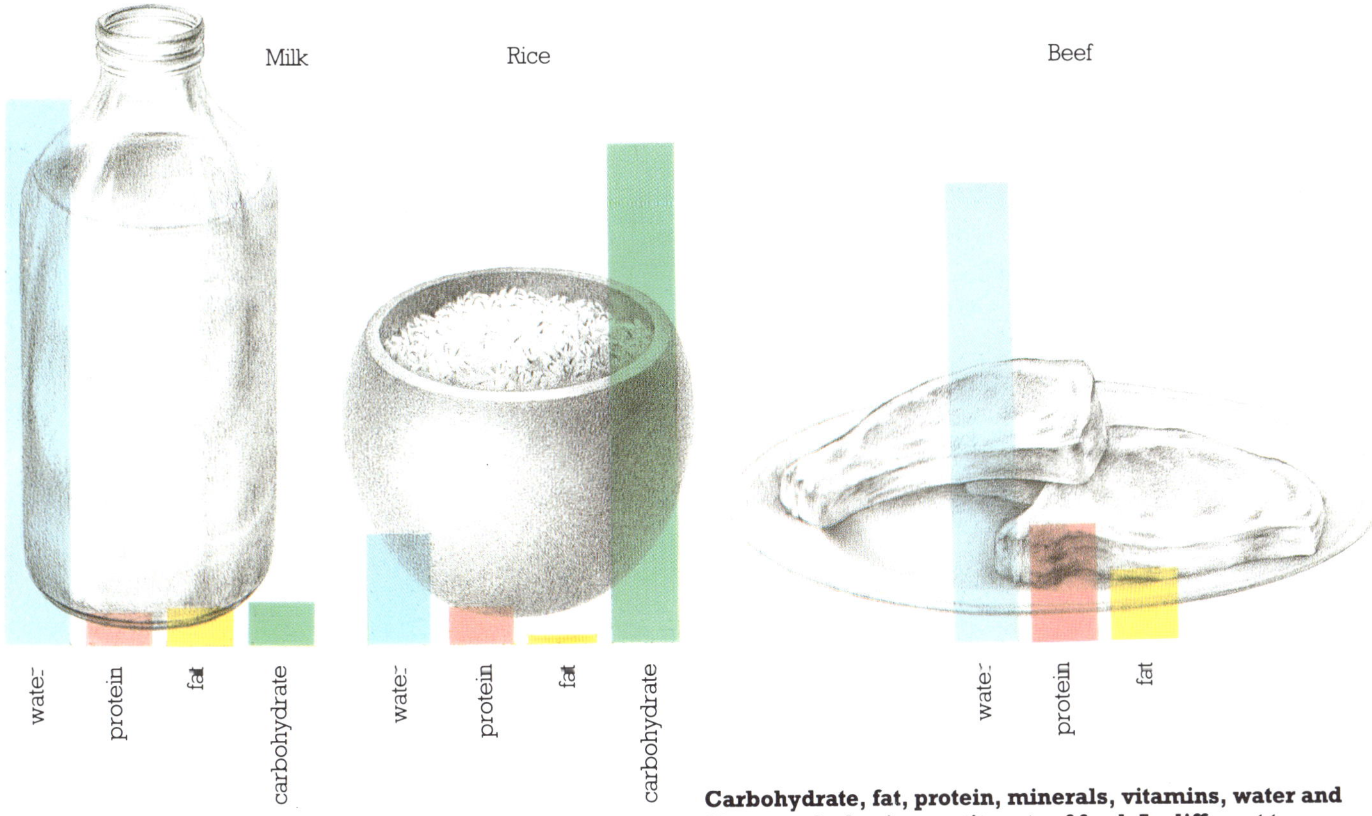

Carbohydrate, fat, protein, minerals, vitamins, water and fibre are the basic constituents of food. In different types of food they are present in different proportions.

Carbohydrates

Carbohydrates contain the chemical elements carbon, hydrogen and oxygen and are used in our bodies as the major fuel for producing energy and for building up new molecules.

There are two main types of carbohydrate. The first type is simple carbohydrates which are small molecules like glucose, fructose (the natural sugar in fruit) and lactose (milk sugar). Ordinary white or brown cane sugar, known as sucrose, is another simple carbohydrate. These are called simple carbohydrates because they are made up of only one or two molecules joined together. Roughly speaking, anything which is very sweet and sugary consists mainly of simple carbohydrate.

The complex carbohydrates are the second type. These are the starchy foods. Complex carbohydrates are made up of many simple carbohydrates linked together. There are three main large carbohydrate molecules; starch, cellulose and glycogen.

Plants store food as starch. Cellulose is also found in plants. The walls of plant cells are made from cellulose. Animals store their carbohydrate as glycogen in their muscles and liver, so glycogen is found in meat and fish. When we eat starch and glycogen, our digestive juices break down these long chains into simple carbohydrates so that they can enter the bloodstream. We cannot digest cellulose, so it stays in our digestive systems. (Fibre, or roughage, consists mainly of plant cellulose.) Our main sources of complex carbohydrates are potatoes, rice, pasta and bread.

It is estimated that we should get about 70% of our energy from complex carbohydrates. We should avoid too many simple carbohydrates because the sugars cause tooth decay and are a very 'instant' source of energy. Whilst this gives our energy levels a boost, it is for a short time and is only useful for short bursts of energy. Complex carbohydrates give us more energy over a length of time. If eaten in excess of energy needs both are stored as glycogen first and, once the glycogen stores are full, the excess will be converted into, and stored as, fat.

Pasta (above right), particularly wholemeal pasta, is a good source of complex carbohydrate whereas sweet drinks (bottom right) consist mostly of simple carbohydrate.

Fibre (Roughage)
Fibre is a mixture of complex carbohydrates. It is made from plant materials like cellulose. Our bodies cannot digest fibre. It is found in unrefined foods, fruit and vegetables. Wholemeal bread, pasta, brown rice, beans and pulses are all excellent sources of fibre.

The digestive system is basically a long tube. Muscles surrounding this tube push the food from the mouth to the anus. Food is mainly digested in the stomach and small intestine and, having been broken down into small molecules, is absorbed into the body from the lower small intestine, the ileum.

Fibre is important in our diets because it keeps the digestive system working efficiently. The remaining substances, the fibre and various waste products (bile pigments) made by the body are moved to the rectum, temporarily stored, then pushed out through the anus.

The muscles which move the food work better if there is enough fibre in the diet to give them more bulk to move along. The waste stays in the body for less time so there is less irritation of the lining of the digestive system. It is estimated that it takes thirty hours for food to travel from mouth to anus in a person with a high fibre diet, but with a low fibre diet the food can take between sixty and ninety hours.

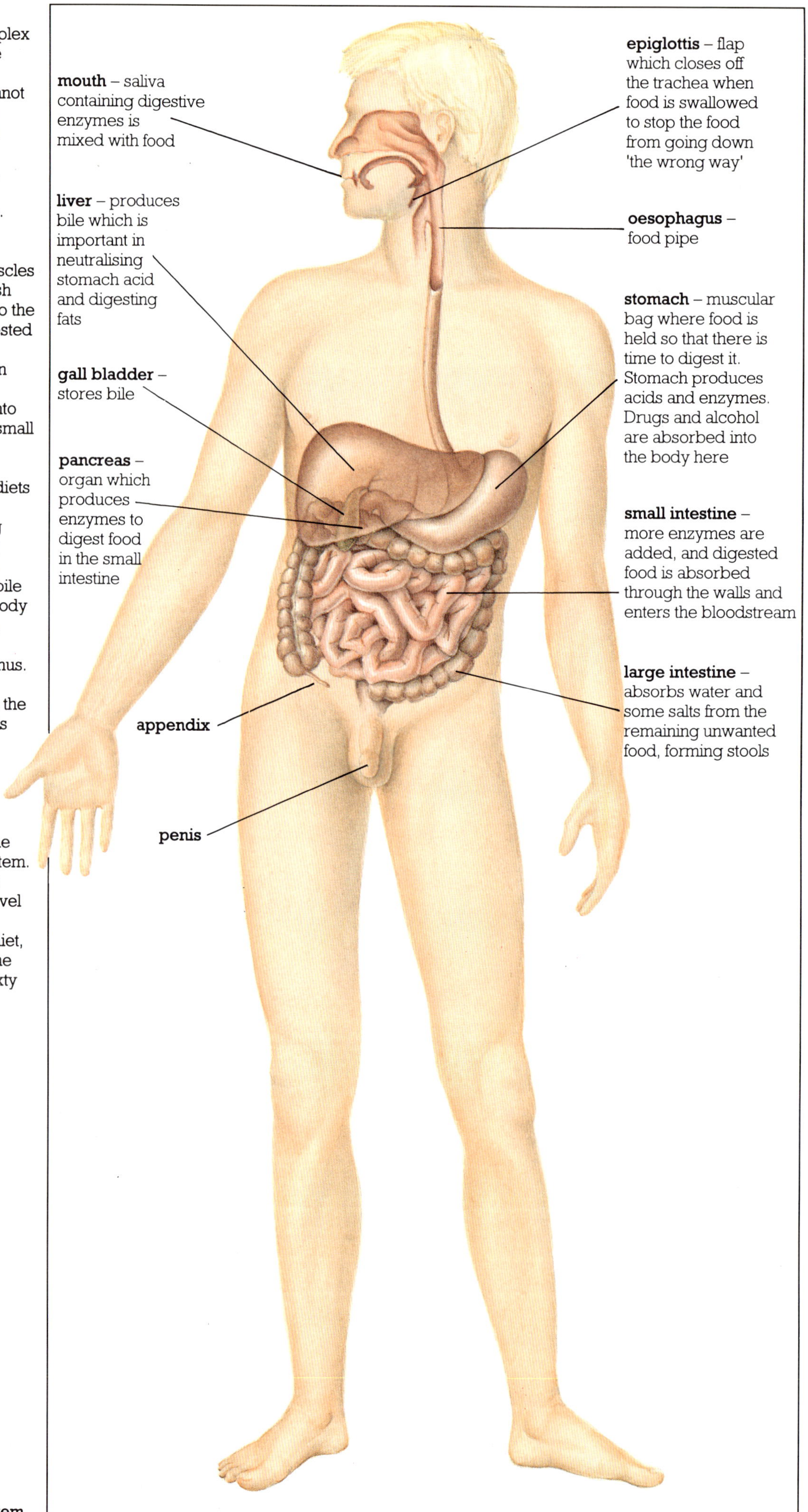

The human digestive system.

Proteins
All proteins are made from small building units called amino acids. Amino acids contain carbon, nitrogen, hydrogen and oxygen, and some contain small amounts of sulphur or phosphorus. Because they contain these extra elements it is essential that we have protein in our diet. Also, as we are unable to store protein, it is important to have a regular supply. Protein is our building material, and we use the protein in our diets to make new cells in order to grow, and to repair and maintain our bodies.

We use about twenty different amino acids and these are linked together to form the different protein molecules needed in our bodies. We must have eight particular amino acids in our diet as we cannot manufacture them, and these are known as the essential amino acids. We are able to use them to make the other twelve. Animal proteins contain all the essential amino acids, but plant proteins do not usually contain all eight. People who do not eat animal products must make sure that they have a varied diet of plant proteins to ensure that they have enough of the essential amino acids.

Fats
Sources of fat include butter, margarine, fried foods, cheeses and meats. Oils are fats which happen to be liquid at room temperature, so that any kind of oil, and food fried in it, will be treated by the body in the same way as fats. Fats, like carbohydrates, contain carbon, hydrogen and oxygen, but the proportion of oxygen is generally very low. Most fats are made up from fatty acids and glycerol.

There are two main types of fat; saturated and unsaturated. The difference is in the structure of the molecules. A saturated fat has its chain of carbon molecules completely full of hydrogen atoms, whereas an unsaturated fat has many fewer hydrogen atoms as a result of a different way of bonding the carbon atoms together. Saturated fats are found in animal products, whereas unsaturated fats are commonly found in vegetable oils and fats.

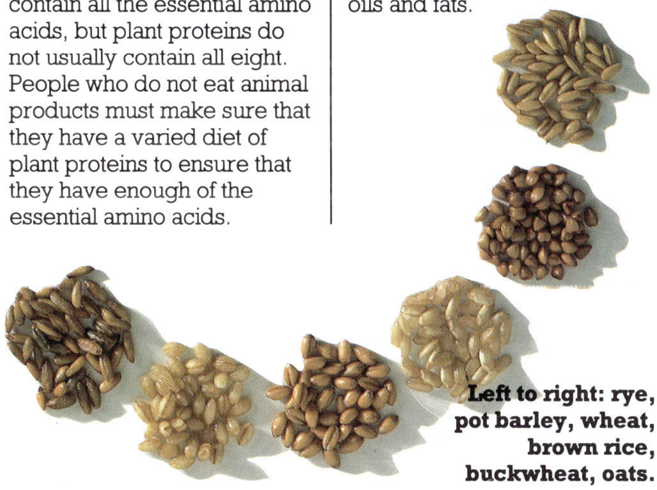

Left to right: rye, pot barley, wheat, brown rice, buckwheat, oats.

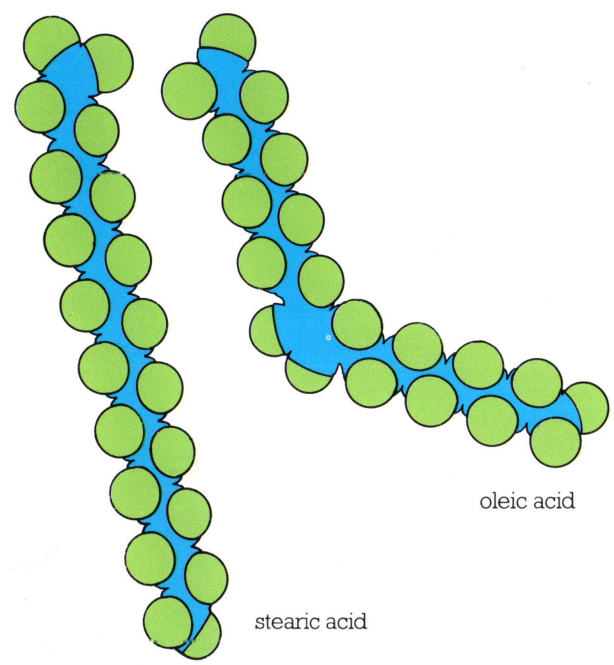

A saturated fat molecule **An unsaturated fat molecule**

Whether a fat is saturated or unsaturated affects its molecular structure, as shown by these space-filling models.

We need some fat in our diet. We are unable to make several important unsaturated fats, so they must be taken in. These are found in most vegetable and seed oils.

Fat is used as a source of energy, when carbohydrate stores run out. It is a useful storage material as it takes up very little room. It is stored around the major organs, where it can also give some protection. It is stored under the skin, too, and can also give some insulation against the cold.

Fat is also necessary in small amounts for healthy growth, and one fat, cholesterol, is needed to make many important hormones, in particular the sex hormones. It is needed, in addition, to keep the membranes of our cells fluid.

Cholesterol, if eaten in excessive quantities, can be harmful. The excess is deposited on the walls of some arteries, and when this occurs it can lead to circulatory problems and, in extreme cases, to a heart attack.

Fish, particularly oily fish, is a good source of unsaturated fat, as well as protein. It is low in saturated fat and eating fish may give us some protection against heart disease.

Research has demonstrated that in men who had already suffered a heart attack, the likelihood of another one was reduced if they ate at least 12 ounces of oily fish each week, or took fish-oil capsules. Three servings a week of such fish as mackerel, herring, fresh sardines, salmon or trout gave maximum protection.

A selection of fresh fish.

MINERALS			
	Average adult male intake in grams/day	**Function**	**Good food sources**
Calcium	1.1	Absence causes rickets.	Dairy products and green vegetables. Calcium is added to all white flour sold in Britain.
Phosphorus	1.4	Needed for energy release in the cells.	Present in nearly all foods.
Sulphur	0.85	Used in making protein.	Protein foods such as meat, fish and eggs.
Potassium	3.3	An essential mineral in all cells and body fluids. Important in nerves.	Vegetables, meat, milk and fruit.
Sodium	4.4	An essential mineral in all cells and body fluids. Used in nerve impulses. Lost from body in sweat.	Salt, bread, cereals, meat products (eg bacon, ham), milk.
Chlorine	5.2	An essential mineral in all cells and body fluids. Lost from body in sweat.	Found in the same foods as sodium. Added to many processed foods.
Magnesium	0.34	Needed in all cells.	Green vegetables.
Iron	0.016	Absence causes anaemia.	Meat and some vegetables. Iron is added to all white flour sold in Britain.
Fluorine (fluoride)	0.0018	Absence may increase dental caries.	Tea, fish bones (in tinned sardines), drinking water, if it has been added.
Iodine	0.0002	Used to make the hormone thyroxine.	Sea-foods, iodized table salt.
Others	There are at least five other trace elements required in minute quantities.		

FAT-SOLUBLE VITAMINS			
Vitamin	Function in the body	Effect of deficiency	Good food sources
A Retinol	Required for night vision. Protects eye surfaces, skin, and lining of airways.	Night blindness, severe eye lesions, can lead to complete blindness.	Fish liver oils, liver, butter, margarine, carrots, dark green vegetables.
D Calciferol	Essential for uptake and use of calcium and phosphorus for healthy bones and strong teeth.	Weak bones which then bend under the weight of the body causing the disease rickets.	Fish liver oils, dairy products. It is made in the skin by the action of sunlight.
K	Involved in the blood clotting process.	Deficiency is unlikely, as it is manufactured by bacteria in the gut.	Spinach, cabbage, cauliflower, peas, cereals.
WATER-SOLUBLE VITAMINS			
B1 Thiamin	Essential for the release of energy from carbohydrates.	Beri beri (nervous paralysis and muscle weakness).	Meat, liver, milk, eggs, wholemeal flour.
B2 Riboflavin	Essential for energy production and use.	Restricted growth and poor skin.	Milk, meat, liver, eggs.
Nicotinic acid (Niacin)	Essential for energy utilisation.	Skin becomes dark and scaly. This is called pellagra.	Meat, cereals, vegetables, milk.
C Ascorbic acid	Maintaining healthy skin, and mucous membranes.	Slow healing of wounds, bleeding from the mucous membranes, especially gums. This disease is called scurvy.	Fresh fruit and vegetables, especially potatoes, green vegetables and citrus fruits.

Minerals

Minerals are elements, such as iron and calcium, which we need in very small quantities for many different purposes. They are found in a variety of foods.

If your diet has not got enough of one of these minerals, you may get a deficiency disease or disorder. The most common deficiency is a lack of iron. This leads to a condition called anaemia. Iron is needed to make haemoglobin, the red oxygen-carrying pigment found in our blood. If you do not have enough iron, you can't make enough red blood cells, and you feel tired. You may look paler than normal. Women are more likely to suffer from anaemia than men because they lose blood regularly when they menstruate. Because you feel tired all the time, your performance generally will suffer. It has been shown that young people who are anaemic do less well at school. If you think that you may be anaemic, make sure that your diet includes plenty of meat or green vegetables.

It is very unlikely that anyone eating a variety of different foods will suffer from a mineral deficiency. Nevertheless mineral supplements are available from health food stores, chemists and supermarkets.

Vitamins

You need a regular but small amount of thirteen vitamins. As with minerals, if you eat a varied diet you are unlikely to have a deficiency.

Humans can make vitamin D. This manufacturing process is activated by the action of the Sun on our skin. People who emigrate to Britain from very sunny countries may be advised to take a vitamin D supplement until their bodies adjust to the less sunny climate of the United Kingdom. Lack of vitamin D stops our bones taking up calcium, so they get soft and, in growing children, are liable to bend. The preparation of food can also substantially reduce the content of some vitamins. Cutting, slicing and grating will all reduce the amount of vitamins in the food. Cooking also destroys vitamins. In general, the fresher the food, the higher the vitamin content.

Many people take vitamin tablets. These can be helpful if you have a poor diet, and are unlikely to be harmful if you follow the manufacturers' recommended doses. Any excess water-soluble vitamins are removed with water in urine. Fat-soluble vitamins are stored in our bodies, and so can actually be toxic (poisonous) if taken in very large quantities.

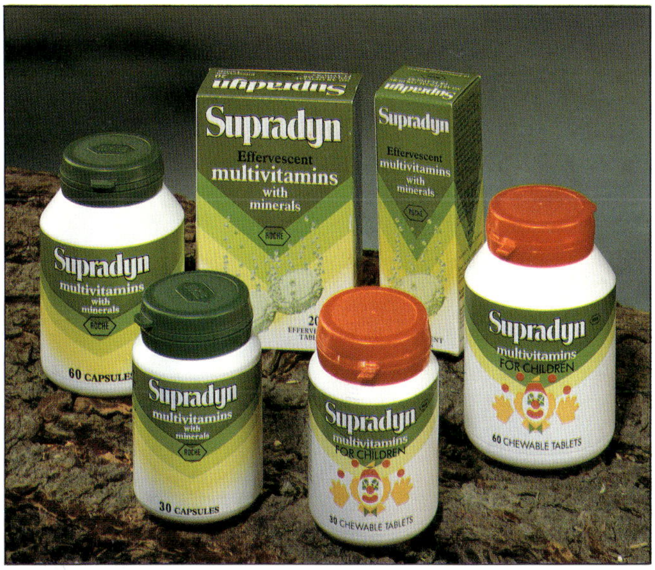

Vitamin tablets are sometimes a useful supplement.

Fresh vegetables and fresh fruit are a good, natural and tasty source of vitamins, minerals and fibre.

Water
About 65% of our bodies is water. Each individual cell can be up to 80% water. All our chemical reactions take place in water, which is found in all foods and drinks. This water is absorbed from the stomach and small intestine. It is important not to allow ourselves to dehydrate because even a 1% drop in our water concentration would leave us feeling very ill indeed. Drinking water after exercising will replace the fluid lost through sweating. If you suffer from a bad bout of diarrhoea, this can lead rapidly to being dehydrated as well. Small babies and young children must be encouraged to drink on very hot days or if they are ill so that they do not lose too much water.

Alcohol
Many people drink lager, beer, wine and spirits as part of their diet. Alcoholic drinks contain varying quantities of ethanol, a chemical made up of carbon, hydrogen and oxygen (formula C_2H_5OH). Alcohol is a powerful drug and changes the way you and your body behave. In small quantities it can be taken up and used as fuel for energy by our muscles, but in excess it is treated as a poison by the body. The liver makes it harmless by breaking it down. The remaining substances are used by the body like a carbohydrate and, taken in excess over the years, can be turned into fat and make you plump or obese.

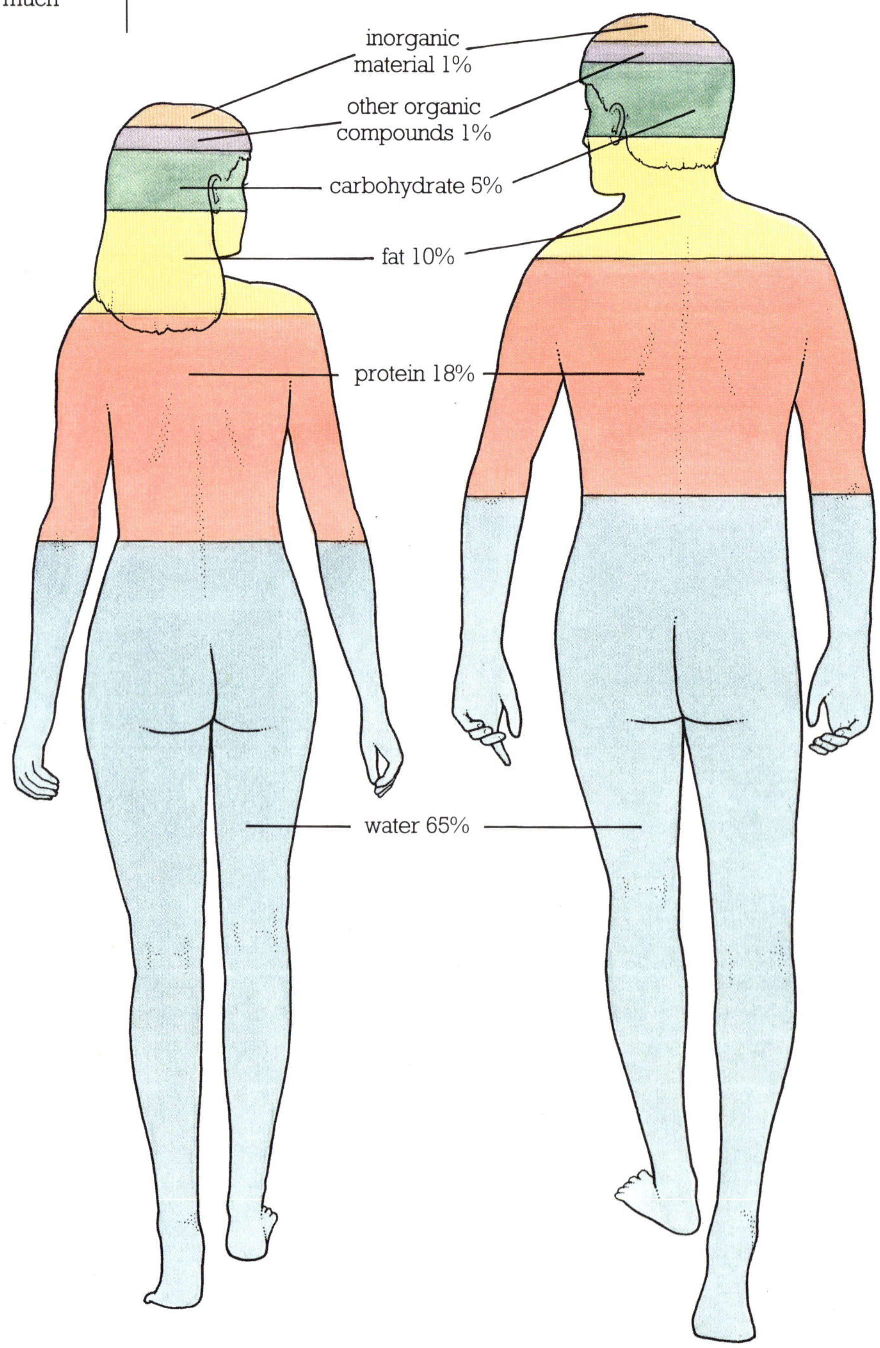

Human beings are mostly water.

A very rough guide is that one unit of alcohol = 1 small glass of wine = 1 small glass of sherry = 1/2 pint of beer/lager = 1/2 glass cider = 1 single measure of spirit = 1/4 pint strong beer/lager

There is no evidence that alcohol taken in small quantities is harmful but it can be harmful if taken regularly in large quantities. Liver cells are destroyed when they are saturated with alcohol. A heavy drinking session can destroy a few hundred liver cells. If this is repeated regularly, the liver can become scarred which leads to cirrhosis, a harmful liver disease. Women should drink less than men and lighter people should drink less than heavy people. This is because of the difference in the amount of blood and body fluids. The less body fluid you have, the more you are affected by alcohol.

The recommended maximum amounts of alcohol are 21 units of alcohol a week for men and 14 units a week for women. Recently, low-alcohol and alcohol-free wines and beers have become increasingly popular. These are useful for people who enjoy a drink but are anxious not to exceed the recommended limits. A recent study has discovered that even pregnant women can drink moderately after the first few weeks of pregnancy without any adverse effect on their babies. They are advised to drink no more than eight units a week after the first few weeks of pregnancy (but none at all if they are trying to conceive, or think that they are just pregnant).

The table above illustrates different ways in which one unit of alcohol can be made up.

Heavy drinking has other adverse effects on your physical health. It can lead to drinkers becoming overweight. Drinking alcohol affects your co-ordination and your ability to concentrate. This can be dangerous if you are in control of machinery or a car, so there are laws which limit how much you may drink before you drive, or operate machinery. It also upsets people's judgement and self-restraint – drunken people are often 'spoiling for a fight', so avoid them.

The penalties for drinking and driving at September 1990 are:

Offence	**Maximum penalty**
Unfit to drive through drink or drugs	£2,000 fine plus 6 months' gaol sentence; disqualification for at least 12 months.
Driving or attempting to drive whilst above the legal limit	£2,000 fine plus 6 months' gaol sentence; disqualification for at least 12 months.
In charge of a vehicle whilst above the legal limit	£1,000 fine plus 3 months' gaol; 10 penalty points or disqualification.

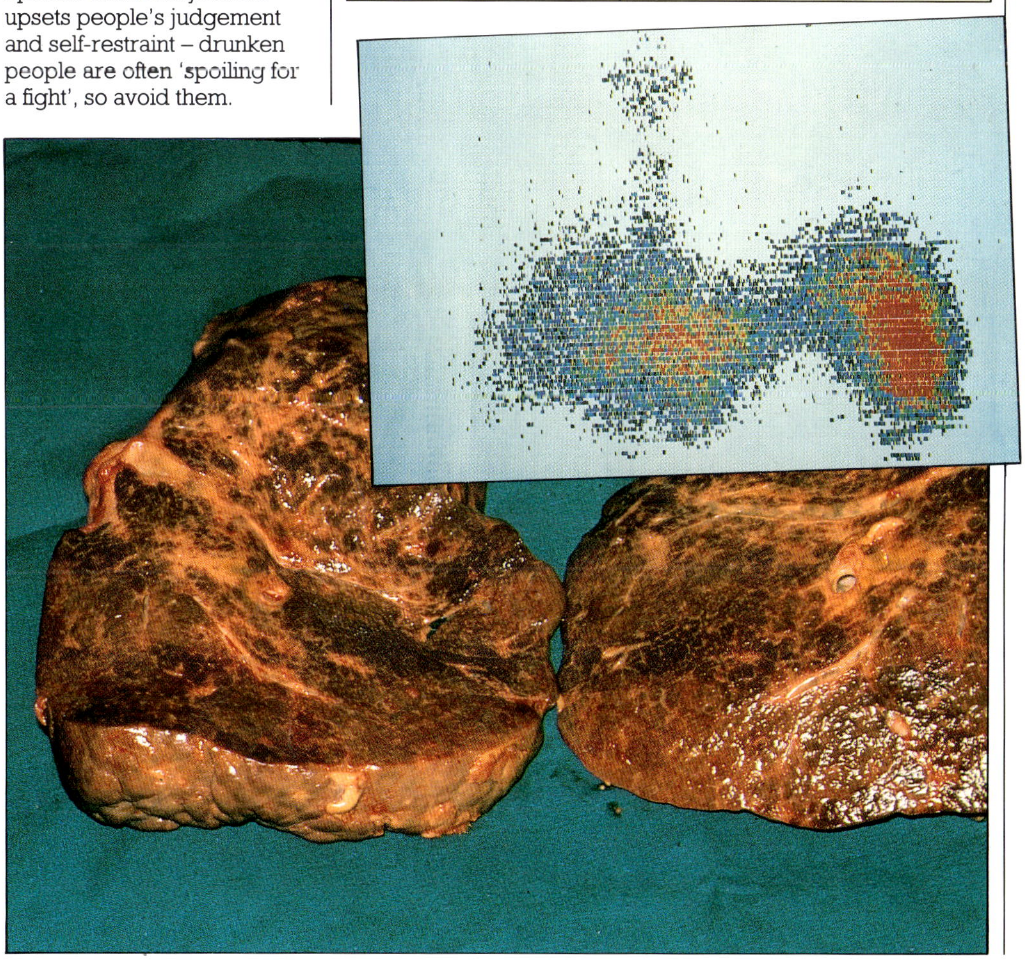

A scintigram and a whole liver from someone with cirrhosis. Cirrhosis can be caused when people drink very heavily over a long period of time.

The food requirements of people in different situations varies. Hard physical work uses up more energy per hour than sedentary work.

TOO MUCH OR TOO LITTLE FOOD?

Another way in which you must balance your diet is to ensure that you have the right amount of energy. Every food has an energy value. If you have too little food, then you will feel weak, and too much food will result in your putting on weight. How much food you can eat depends on several things.

● Size. In general, the taller and heavier you are, the more food you need.

● Gender. Men need more food than women.

● Amount of work/exercise. If you lead a very active life, then you will be using more energy. Food is used as a fuel for this energy, so you will need more food.

● Metabolic rate. Even if you are not exercising, you still need a certain amount of energy to keep your body processes going. The rate at which your body burns up food is called your metabolic rate. The rate at which people use up food varies. The rate will depend on many things – how much lean muscle tissue you have, your rate of growth and many other factors. This explains why two people can lead identical lifestyles, eat the same, yet one can put on weight whilst the other may even lose weight.

It is not healthy to be either seriously underweight or overweight. Being obese (more than 20% overweight) can lead to circulatory problems. Your heart will not increase in size in proportion to your body weight, so your heart has to do more work in pumping the blood around a bigger body. Blood pressure is likely to be higher in overweight people and high blood pressure can have serious consequences. Blood pressure invariably goes down when fat people lose weight.

IMPROVING YOUR DIET

Most diets do not need changing. However, studying typical Western diets and comparing them with diets from other areas of the world has shown several differences. These differences also tend to correlate to the incidence of certain diseases which are common in countries like ours, whereas they are comparatively rare elsewhere.

Recommendations are:

● Take care how much fat you eat. About 40–45% of most people's energy comes from fat. Experts think that this is much too high and should be reduced to less than 30%. Too much fat, especially saturated fats, can lead to atherosclerosis. This is where fat deposits on the walls of arteries, causing them to narrow. This means that the heart has to work harder to pump the blood around the body. Sometimes, the arteries narrow so much over the years that they become blocked. This can be fatal.

To avoid this, eat less fried food. Grill and bake food instead of frying it, cut off all visible fat from meat, eat poultry and fish rather than red meats, eat cheese sparingly, use low fat substitutes like yoghurt or fromage frais instead of cream and low fat spread instead of butter or margarine. Adults could drink skimmed or semi-skimmed milk. (Young children should have full cream milk as their nutritional requirements are very different.) Cut down on high fat snacks like crisps and nuts.

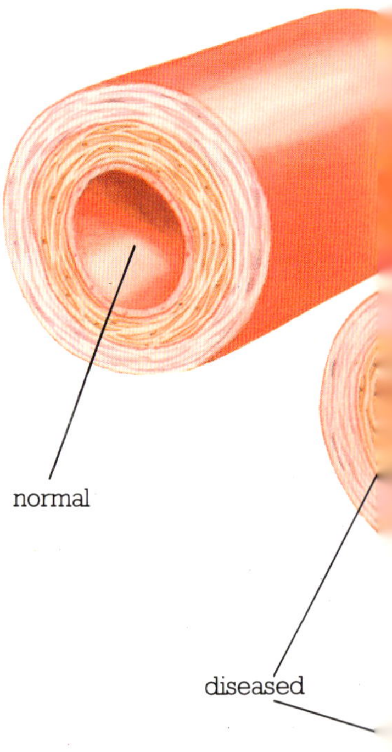

● Eat few simple carbohydrates. Try to cut down on sweet, sugary foods. They are very bad for your teeth, causing decay. Bacteria living in plaque on your teeth act on the sugar in your food, turning it to acid, which starts to eat away at your tooth enamel. Cutting down the amount of time in which your teeth are in contact with sugar is the best way of avoiding decay. Regular brushing also helps to get rid of plaque.

● Eat less salt unless it is hot and you are sweating a lot. Then you may need extra salt to replace what you lose in sweat. Too much salt can raise blood pressure. To cut down on the amount of salt, you can use less in cooking. Don't add any extra when the food is on your plate. Cut down on salted snacks.

● Eat plenty of complex carbohydrates. This is achieved by eating more rice, pasta, bread and potatoes. Experts think that we should be getting at least 50%–70% of our energy from these carbohydrates. Our diet would be further improved if we ate the wholemeal, unrefined versions of these foods.

Eating too much fat, smoking and taking no exercise can lead to heart disease. In these people the heart's arteries become 'furred up' and the heart has to work harder to force blood through the narrowing arteries.

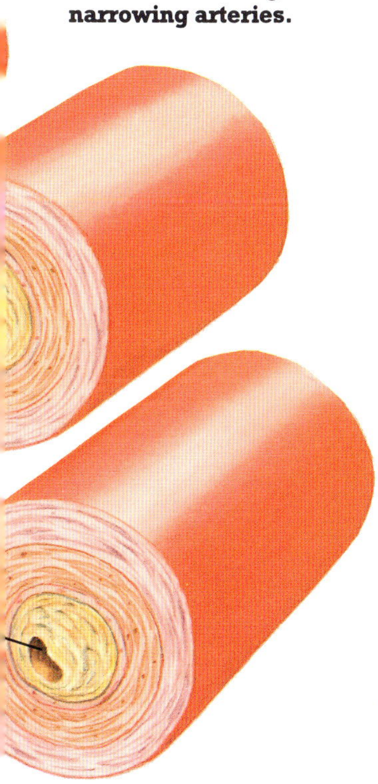

● Eat plenty of fibre. Eating more fibre will prevent constipation and lower the chance of getting bowel cancer and other bowel diseases. In addition to foods rich in complex carbohydrates, fruit and vegetables, as well as beans, are all excellent sources of fibre.

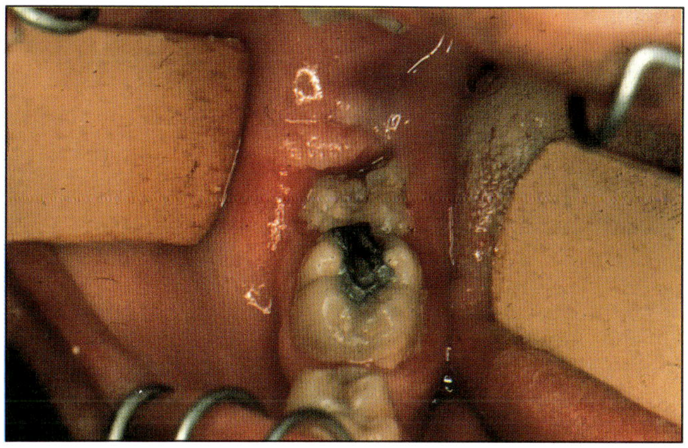

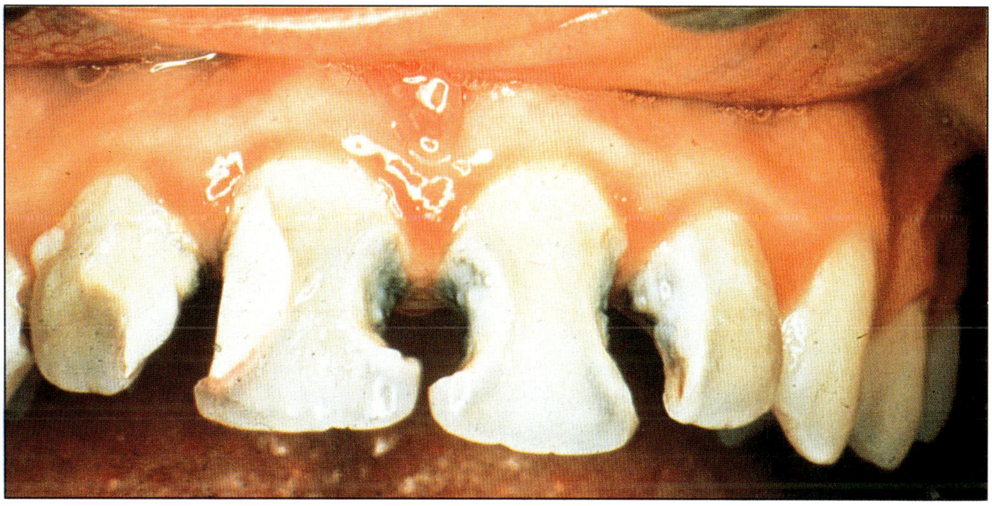

Eating too much sugary food and not taking good care of our teeth can have painful consequences.

DIET AND CANCER

There have been many links between diet and cancers of different types. Some experts say that between one-third and a half of all cancers in the UK and North America are linked to what people eat. Many of the recommendations for improving your diet will reduce your chances of developing cancer.

Other recommendations are:

- Wash all fruit and vegetables to remove any chemicals, eg pesticides.
- Eat fewer smoked and cured meats; these are high in nitrates and nitrites which are added during their preparation.
- Keep cling film made from PVC away from direct contact with fatty foods like butter. Some of the chemicals are leached into the food.
- Avoid foods with many artificial additives.

This advice is being given because it is thought that many chemicals act as carcinogens (cancer-causing substances). By cutting down the number of chemicals added to our foods, we are less likely to expose our digestive systems to carcinogens. All chemicals are carefully checked before they are used, but the incidence of cancers of the digestive system are much lower in countries where they eat plenty of vegetable fibre and foods without any chemicals added.

DIFFERENT DIETS

There are many different kinds of diet. Diets vary from country to country and from person to person. What we should all strive for is a balanced diet. There are so many different foods to choose from, it is possible to achieve a balance in many different ways. For example, if you lived on sardine and water cress sandwiches, you would be eating a balanced diet, but a very restricted one.

RESTRICTED DIETS

Many people restrict their diets. Some are restricted by religious laws. Others choose not to eat certain types of food. For example, vegetarians choose not to eat meat. This may be simply because they don't like meat, or they disagree with the way that animals bred for consumption are treated, or they believe eating meat is wasteful in terms of the planet's resources. Having a restricted diet does not mean that you can't have a more balanced diet than those meat-eaters who miss out fresh fruit and vegetables. In fact, many vegetarians have a much healthier diet. The incidence of many diet-related diseases is much lower in vegetarians than in meat-eaters; for example, vegetarians tend to have a lower incidence of heart disease and cancer of the colon, they are less likely to be overweight, they tend to have lower cholesterol levels and to suffer far less from constipation. Major reasons for these differences could be a much higher fibre intake from the vegetables and fewer saturated fats from animal products.

An even more restricted diet is that of vegans. Vegans are very strict vegetarians who will not eat any animal product at all, including all dairy products and eggs. Care has to be taken to ensure an adequate intake of calcium, iron, zinc and vitamin B12, as well as taking in a rich variety of plant proteins to ensure that the eight essential amino acids are included in the vegan diet.

3: LUNGS FOR LIFE

We breathe because we need the oxygen from the air to enable us to release energy from the food we eat. Our lungs, together with an efficient circulatory transport system, make sure that we get oxygen to every cell in our body. Our rate of breathing depends on how much energy we need and how healthy our lungs are.

We need oxygen to produce energy which we then use for many different activities, like moving, keeping warm, growing – thinking, too, requires a small supply of energy. The process that produces the body's energy is called respiration and it takes place in every cell in our body. It involves the use of oxygen to break down some of the food we eat, for example, glucose, with the release of energy and the formation of carbon dioxide and water as waste products.

GLUCOSE + OXYGEN —> ENERGY + CARBON DIOXIDE + WATER

The energy released by the 'oxidation' of food does not directly supply our bodies. It is used to build up molecules of a substance called adenosine triphosphate (ATP) in our cells.

ATP is made up of an adenosine part, which has attached to it three phosphate groups. An enzyme (biological catalyst) called ATPase changes ATP into adenosine diphosphate (ADP) by splitting off one of the three phosphate groups. When this happens, a lot of energy is released from the ATP molecule.

ATP has been found in all cells and is believed to be the ready energy supply for all living things. Cell respiration provides the energy so that ADP is constantly being changed back into ATP and supplies don't run out. At any given time, there is only about 50g of ATP in an adult's body, although thousands of times that amount is made in a day to provide energy.

The first fuel for cell respiration is glucose carried in the blood. If this runs out, then carbohydrate reserves, stored as glycogen in the liver and muscles, are converted into glucose to be used. When the carbohydrate store has

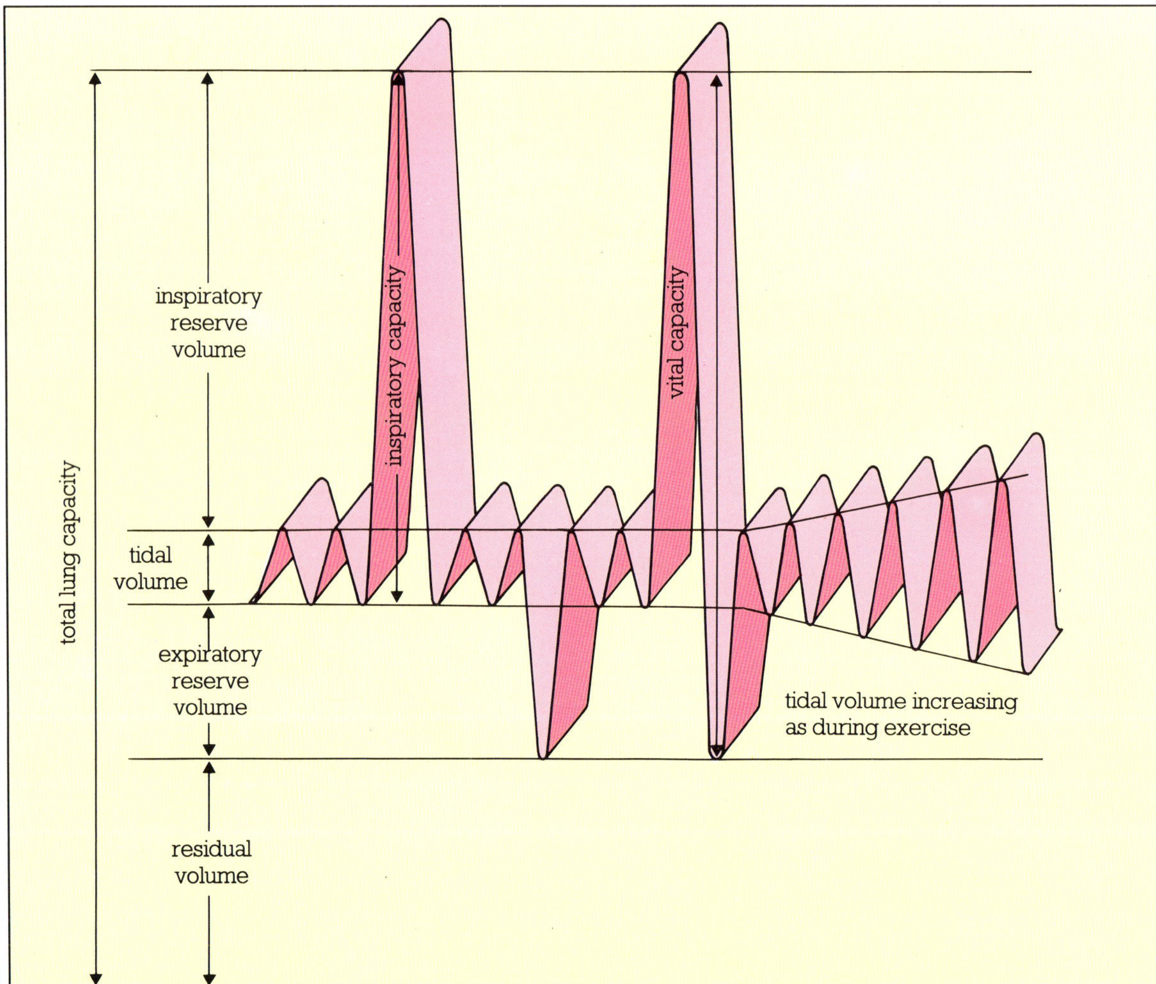

TIDAL VOLUME
This is the amount of air normally breathed in and out during a single breath by a resting person.

INSPIRATORY RESERVE VOLUME
This is the extra amount of air you can breathe in over and above the tidal volume.

EXPIRATORY RESERVE VOLUME
This is the maximum amount of air you can breathe out over and above the tidal volume.

VITAL CAPACITY
This is the amount of air exhaled during a maximum expiration following a maximum inspiration (that is the biggest amount of air you can breathe in).

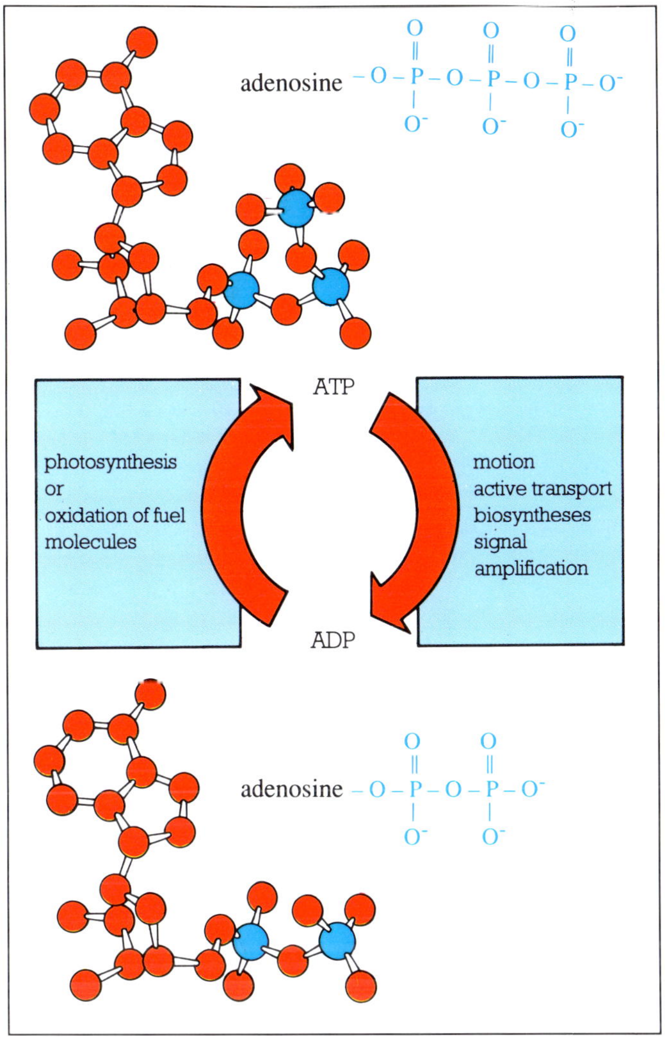

been used, fat will be broken down and oxidised. In starvation, protein will also be used as a source of energy.

By breathing, we not only take in the oxygen which we need, we also get rid of the waste products of respiration. We breathe out carbon dioxide and water vapour. As a result, the relative proportions of the gases found in inhaled air (air we breathe in) and in exhaled air (air we breathe out) are different.

We call breathing in inspiration and breathing out expiration.

MEASURING RESPIRATORY VOLUMES
The volume of air which we breathe in and out can be measured by using a spirometer. From the measurements made we can work out tidal volume, inspiratory reserve volume, expiratory reserve volume and vital capacity. These are explained in the graph on page 20.

Residual volume cannot be measured by a spirometer, as it is the amount of air left in the lungs even after carrying out a maximum expiration.

(Above) The ATP – ADP cycle is the basic mode of energy exchange in biological systems.

(Right) Fat and carbohydrate; their use in aerobic and anaerobic respiration.

If you are using a lot of energy, you have to breathe more often, and deeper, in order to get enough oxygen to your working cells, so the amount of air breathed in and out in one breath (ie tidal volume) increases.

Even if your breathing rate increases considerably, there is a limit to how much oxygen your body can take up. This can be measured by analysing the air which you breathe out as you do some progressive exercise, for example, running on a treadmill the speed of which gradually increases, or on a bicycle machine where the resistance can be altered. When the concentration of oxygen expired remains constant, your body is taking up as much as it can. This measurement is known as your VO_2 maximum, or maximal oxygen uptake. It is basically a measure of how much oxygen your lungs can take up per minute.

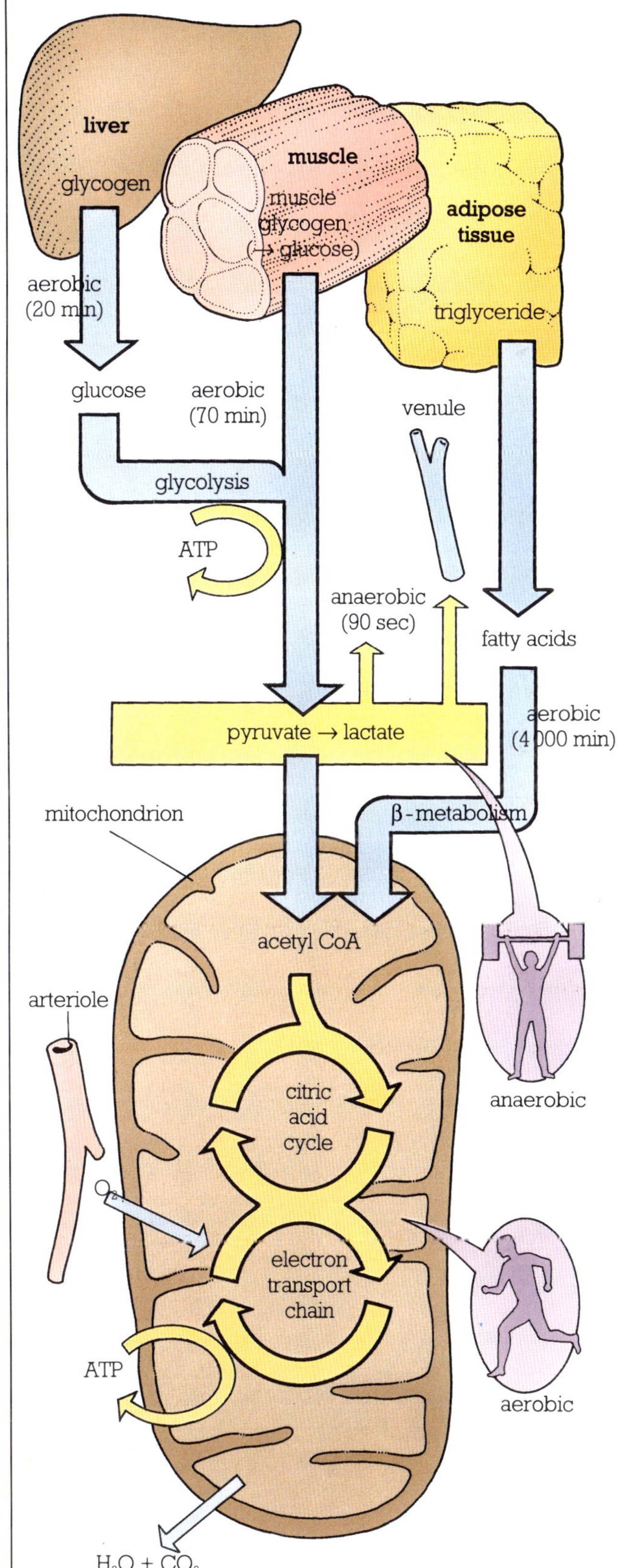

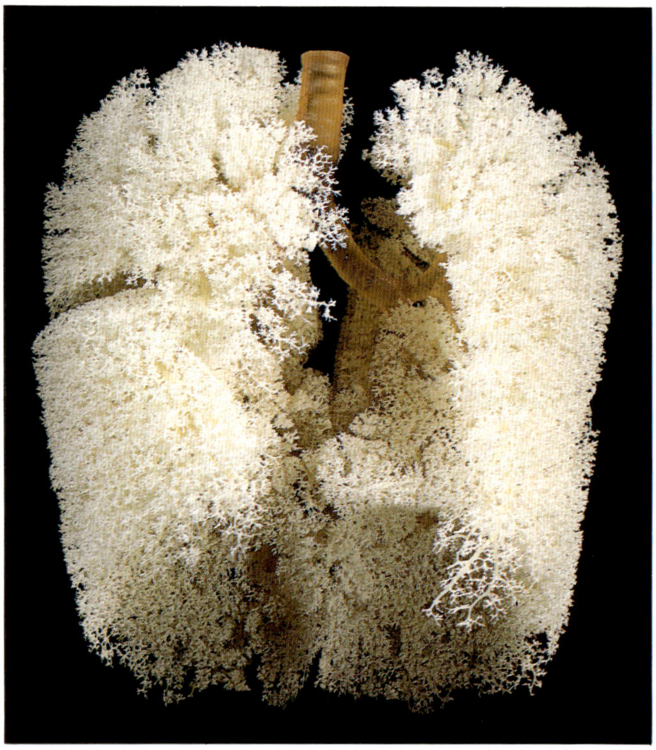

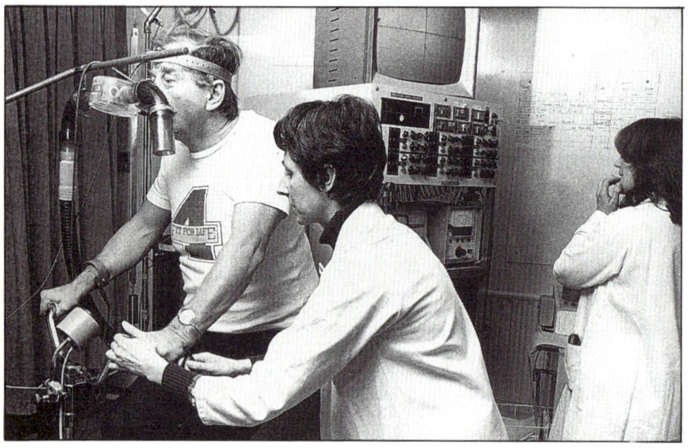

(Above left) A cast of the lungs.

(Above) A cast of the blood vessels in the lungs.

(Left) The VO_2 max test in progress.

$$C_6H_{12}O_6 \rightarrow 2CH_3CH(OH)COOH$$

GLUCOSE → LACTIC ACID

Sometimes you need to produce energy when there is very little oxygen available. To provide this energy, your body can respire anaerobically, that is without oxygen, for a short time. Lactic acid is produced as a waste product.

There is much less energy produced from anaerobic respiration – less than one-tenth of the energy produced from full aerobic respiration (with oxygen). This is because there is a lot of energy still contained in the lactic acid. If the level of lactic acid builds up, it can stop the muscle working effectively. Lactic acid is broken down when oxygen becomes available again.

If you have been exercising, you continue to breathe quickly for several minutes after you stop. This is to pay off the oxygen debt which your body has produced by using all available oxygen and then respiring anaerobically and making lactic acid. Gentle warm-down exercise, like jogging a few hundred metres will help to pay off the debt by keeping the breathing rate higher and keeping a good circulation of blood rich in oxygen going to the working muscles.

THE MECHANICS OF BREATHING

To understand how we breathe, it is necessary to look at the structure of our respiratory system. Our lungs are found in our thoracic cavity.

Air is warmed, filtered and moistened in the nostrils. It then travels down the trachea, which is supported by incomplete rings of cartilage (gristle) to stop it collapsing. The air then goes into the bronchi, and gaseous diffusion occurs between this air and that remaining in the alveoli (air sacs). There, the oxygen in the air dissolves in the moist lining, and moves into the circulatory system through the alveolar walls. Oxygen moves by a process known as diffusion, a general term for the movement of a substance from an area of high concentration to an area of low concentration. As there is more oxygen in the lungs than in the blood, the molecules move across. Carbon dioxide moves from the blood to the lungs by the same process. The concentrations will always be different as the blood is constantly moving, and taking away all the oxygen which has diffused across.

The human respiratory system.

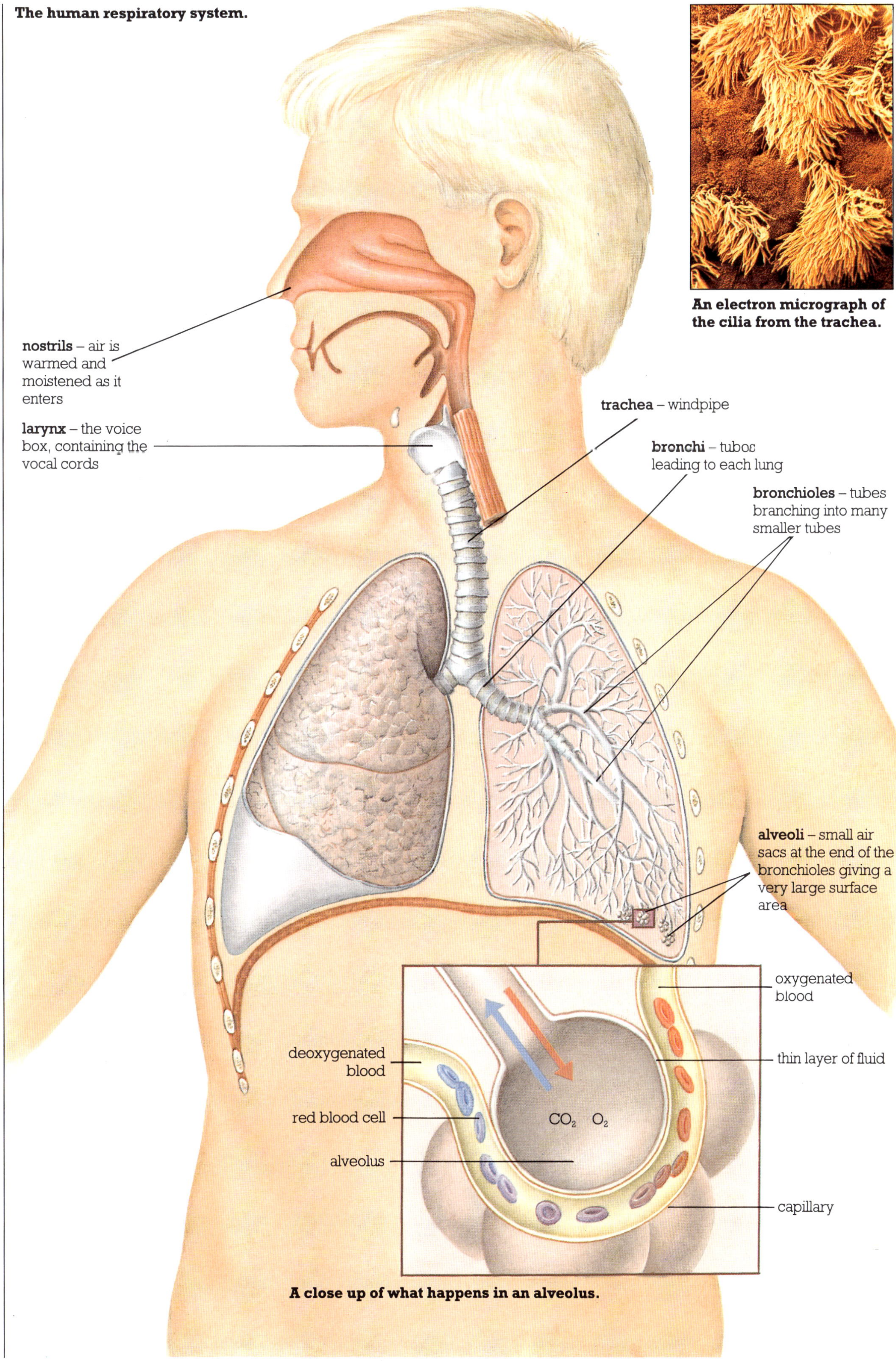

An electron micrograph of the cilia from the trachea.

A close up of what happens in an alveolus.

BREATHING IN	BREATHING OUT
External intercostal muscles pull the ribs up and out	External intercostal muscles relax and ribs fall down and in*
Diaphragm muscles contract, pulling diaphragm flat	Diaphragm muscles relax. Diaphragm returns to dome shaped
Volume increases	Volume decreases
Pressure drops	Pressure increases
Air enters the lungs	Air leaves the lungs

*During rapid or forced breathing, the internal intercostal muscles pull the ribs down and in. This is quicker than letting them fall under their own weight.

In order to get the air inside the lungs, the ribs and diaphragm change the volume of the thoracic cavity causing a lowering of pressure so that air from the atmosphere enters through the nose and mouth. The events are summarised in the table above.

The lungs are covered by the pleural membranes which are lubricated and normally slide over each other at every breath. This reduces the friction between the lungs and the ribs.

The rate of breathing is controlled by a specialised part of the brain stem (the medulla). The rate responds to changes in carbon dioxide concentration in the blood and to messages received from various receptors.

Sometimes there are abnormal breathing patterns. One such abnormality is hyperventilation. Hyperventilation occurs during vigorous exercise, when oxygen requirements rise. During rest, hyperventilation can occur and results in a quickened breathing rate and often in a feeling of dizziness and cramp.

Asthma is a disorder caused by the small bronchioles in the lungs going into spasm. These small tubes have muscular walls which contract during an attack. This, together with the mucus found in the lungs, makes it difficult for the sufferer to breathe normally. The trigger for an attack can be anything – an infection, stress, or even changes in the weather. Once diagnosed, asthma is now more easily controlled than it was in the past. Inhalers containing bronchodilators offer immediate relief from an asthma attack by relaxing the muscles and unblocking the airways. Low dosage steroid based drugs can reduce the probability of severe attacks if they are taken regularly.

Once asthma has been diagnosed and controlled, most asthmatics can lead a full life. Having asthma shouldn't prevent people from enjoying sport – even at a high level. Ian Botham, David Wilkie and Liz Hobbs are all top-class athletes who cope with asthma.

KEEPING THE LUNGS CLEAN

There are many airborne microbes which cause disease. To avoid infections, the lungs have a defence system.

Air entering into the nose is moistened and warmed and hairs inside the nostrils filter out the large particles of dust and dirt.

The trachea has goblet cells which produce a clear fluid called mucus. Small particles stick to the fluid, which is then moved by tiny paddle-like outgrowths of the cells lining the trachea, called cilia. The mucus is swept up to the back of the throat and swallowed.

CASE HISTORY

As World, European and British Waterski racing champion Speed Record Holder and Waterski Personality of the Year 1982, Liz Hobbs has refused to allow asthma to affect her sporting career. She regards her childhood experience of being obliged to forgo P.E. and games at school as the basis of her determination to succeed in waterskiing, which she discovered at the age of nine.

Liz says, 'Some of the best potential is to be found in an asthmatic. Because that child has had to fight for his or her own breath, he or she could become a natural fighter, a natural athlete or a success at something else.'

Pollution
Breathing polluted air can harm your lungs. Nitrogen oxides from exhaust fumes can inflame the trachea and bronchi and so can sulphur oxides. Carbon monoxide combines with the oxygen-carrying red blood cells so that less oxygen can be carried. Some hydrocarbons are thought to be carcinogenic (cancer producing) and, if inhaled, can be a cause of lung cancer. Working and living in dusty environments can lead to large particles settling in the smaller airways, with the smaller ones even finding their way to the alveoli.

The effects of smoking
Smoke from cigarettes, cigars and pipes contains irritant smoke particles, nicotine (a highly addictive stimulant drug), carbon monoxide and tar which contains carcinogenic hydrocarbons. The adverse effects of smoking are therefore much greater than anything caused by atmospheric pollution.

The irritants in smoke inflame the air passages, making you cough. The goblet cells become enlarged and over-produce mucus. Cilia are temporarily paralysed by smoke so that they cannot move the smoke-laden mucus, and then the only way to move it is by coughing. If you persist in smoking, the cilia shrivel and eventually disappear completely. The lungs cannot defend themselves and are then much more susceptible to infection.

Nicotine is a stimulant to the brain. It also speeds up heart rate and it is highly addictive. This makes it very difficult to give up smoking once you start.

Respiratory function has been measured in a random sample of the population of England and Wales, and found to decline with age from 25 years. At all ages the values were lowest in regular smokers, and highest in life-long non-smokers with ex-smokers between the two levels.

Smoking and fitness
It is much more difficult to sustain a level of fitness if you are a smoker as your oxygen carrying capacity is reduced. There are several reasons for this:

1. It requires more effort for a smoker to breathe. This is because there is an increased resistance to airflow in the smaller air tubes, and it is, therefore, more difficult for the air to get in.

2. The oxygen-carrying pigment, haemoglobin, found in the red blood cells, will pick up the highly poisonous gas carbon monoxide more readily than oxygen. Carbon monoxide is found in the smoke from cigarettes. In a heavy smoker this can mean that the red blood cells only carry 90% of the oxygen carried in the red blood cells of a non-smoker.

3. For the reasons already given, smokers may have lower maximal oxygen consumption. This means that they will get out of breath more quickly when exercising.

4. The nicotine in the cigarette will raise the resting heart rate by as much as 20% for twenty minutes even after just two puffs. Therefore the smoker's heart is already working harder than it needs, even before exercising.

The long-term effects of smoking
If you persist in smoking, it is likely that you will become addicted to the nicotine in cigarettes, and it will be very difficult to give up smoking. It will also mean that if you try, your body will develop withdrawal symptoms like headaches and stomach-aches, and you will become bad tempered, irritable and often edgy whilst your body struggles to manage without this drug.

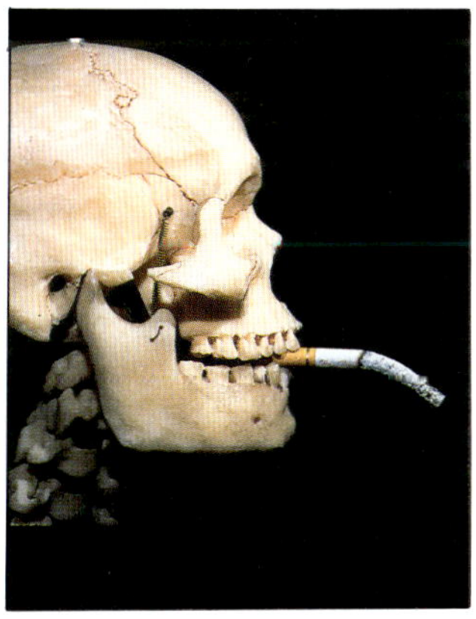

As the cilia are destroyed by the smoke, the lungs are more susceptible to common infections like coughs and colds. Smokers are also more likely to get more serious diseases, such as pneumonia. As the cilia remove the mucus, if they are destroyed there will be a big build up of mucus which can only be removed by coughing: it is little wonder that smokers have a permanent cough.

Heavy smoking damages the breathing system. Serious diseases like emphysema, bronchitis and lung cancer are far more common in smokers. These diseases are all unpleasant and can be fatal.

There is also a link between smoking and the incidence of heart disease. About 180 000 people die in Britain each year from smoking-related heart disease. Smoking also slows down the circulation of the blood, which can cause circulatory disorders. Smoking and health do not go together.

Tobacco consumption in the UK between 1890 and 1980. The traces show the average number of cigarettes smoked per person per day for men and women. (Data from Tobacco Advisory Council).

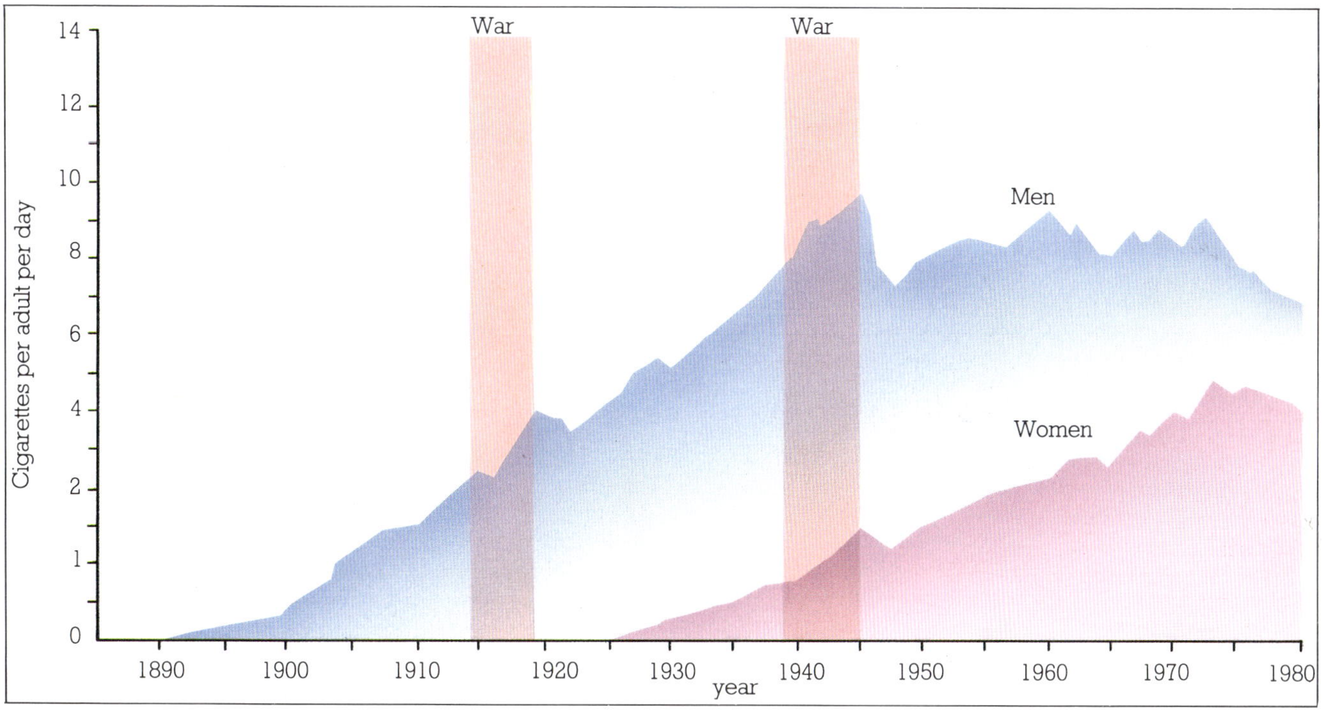

4: EXERCISE FOR HEALTH

One way of improving our physical health is by exercise. Exercise involves using our muscles to move our bones. To do this, we need energy. The fuel which provides the energy comes from the food we eat. This and the oxygen which we need to release the energy is delivered to our muscles by our circulatory system.

HOW WE MOVE

We move by using muscles. The muscles pull on the bones of our skeleton. Bone provides our bodies with support. Our skeleton is made up of many bones meeting at joints, and allows for a wide range of movement.

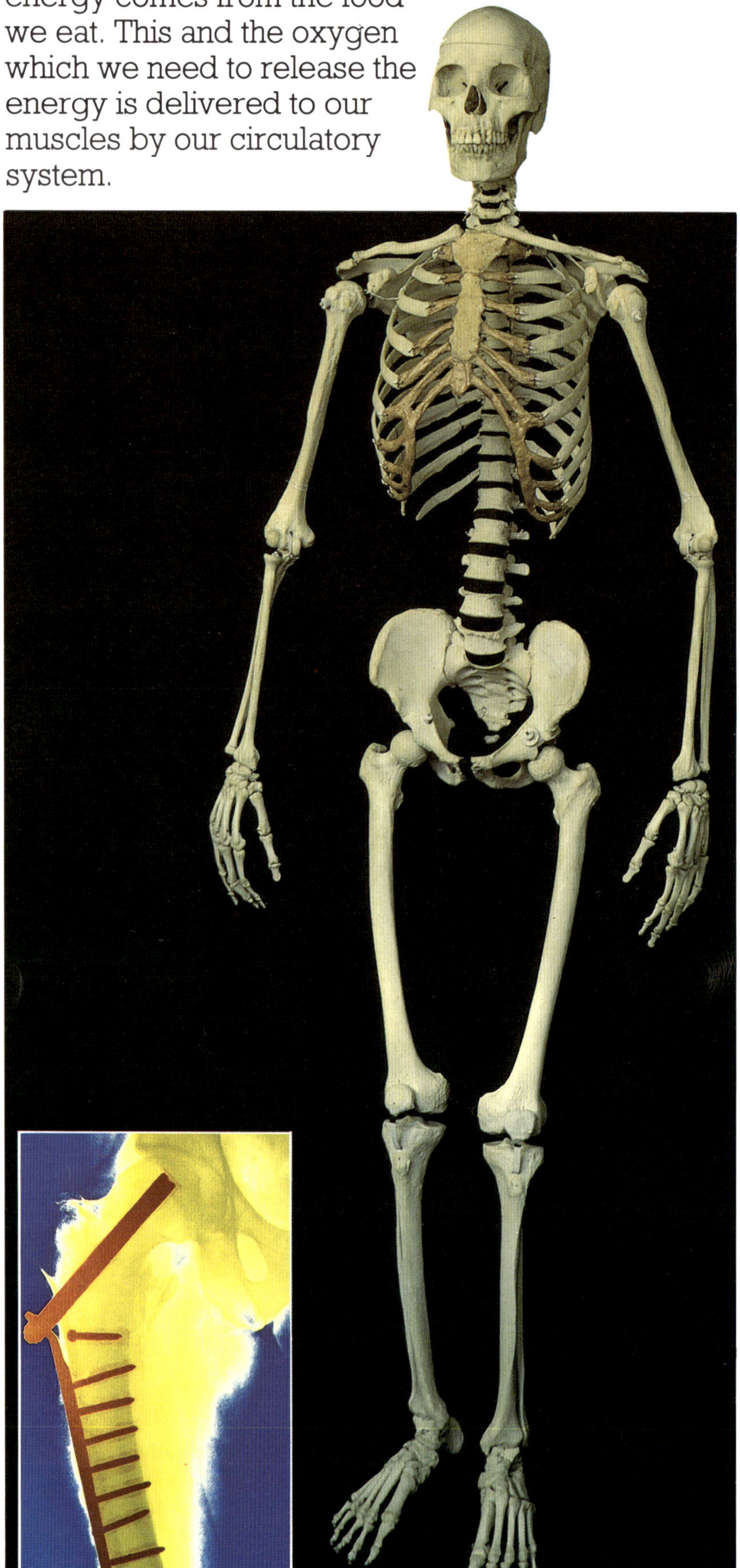

Bones are living tissue; bones consist of protein fibres which give them strength, and minerals like calcium phosphate which make them hard. Like other tissues, bones have a good blood supply and can repair themselves. If you break or crack a bone, the surgeon will set the bone in its original position, and a plaster cast may be used to maintain its position whilst it heals. If the bone has been shattered, pins may be used to hold the parts together as they mend.

Bone is hard, but it is not very flexible. This means that it does not absorb shocks, and can be damaged. Cartilage, a white, tough, flexible substance, stops a lot of this damage. It acts as a shock absorber at the ends of the bones. Babies and young children have a higher proportion of cartilage than adults.

Ligaments hold the bones together at joints. They are made of elastic tissue. It is this elasticity which prevents some injury, as ligaments are able to cushion some shocks by giving slightly.

The human skeleton.

(Inset) A badly broken bone needs pins to hold the parts together as they mend.

Joints are very important as they allow us to make many different movements. Most of the joints concerned with movement are synovial joints. These contain a small amount of fluid which lubricates the joint and enables the bones to move over each other. The fluid is enclosed in the synovial capsule. It is important to keep joints supple for exercise. As people get older, sometimes their joints become inflamed. This is known as arthritis, and can be very painful.

Bones are moved by muscles. Muscles are attached to bones by tendons. Tendons are made from very strong but comparatively inelastic tissue. The small amount of elasticity is used to store energy, so that movement is very efficient,

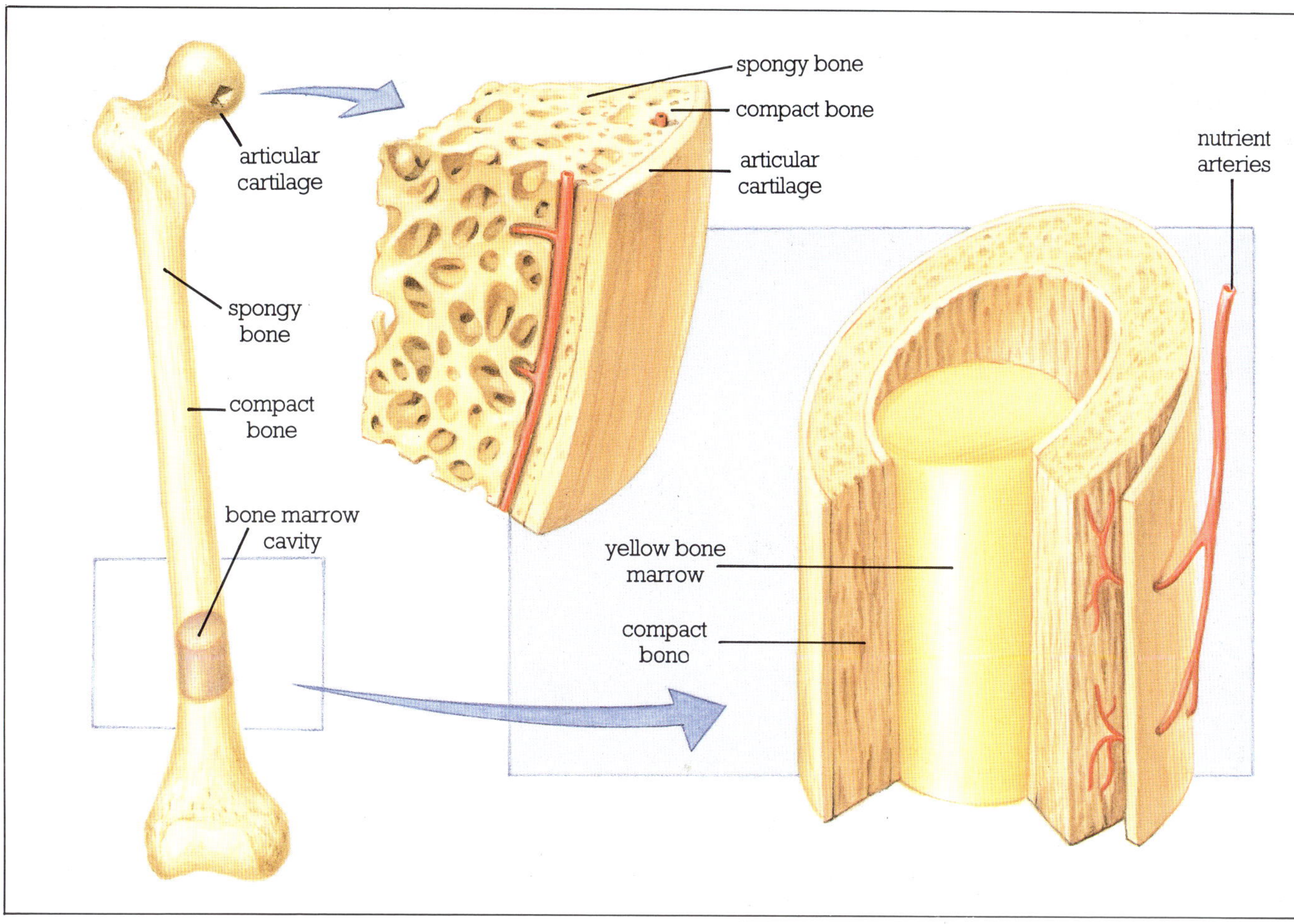

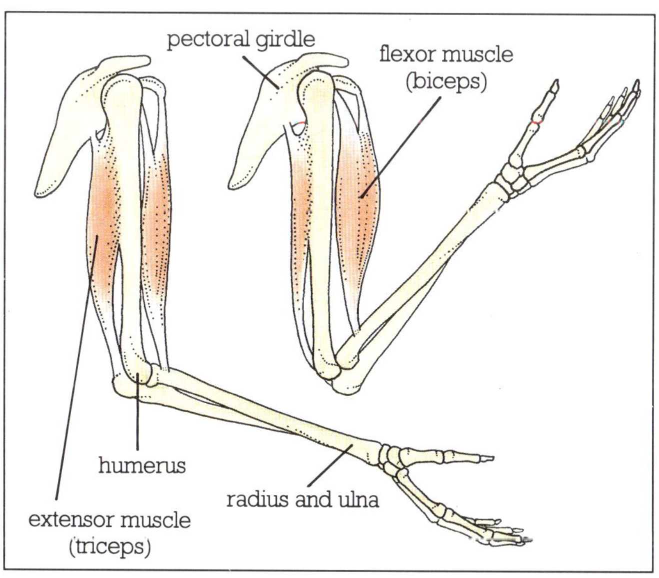

and muscle tearing is prevented. Tendons are surrounded by sheaths of membrane, similar to the membranes found in joints, which enable the tendon fibres to move smoothly as the muscles contract. When a tendon sheath is damaged and becomes inflamed, movement can become painful as the tendon cannot move through it easily.

Muscles work by contracting and pulling on bones. They can't push, so that if a bone is moved, another muscle has to return it to its original place.

Bending (flexing) and straightening (extending) the forearm.

Muscles usually work in pairs, with opposing actions. As one muscle contracts, the other relaxes and is stretched. Pairs of muscles are called antagonistic, or opposing pairs.

Muscles which bend a limb at a joint are called flexor muscles, and muscles which straighten limbs are known as extensor muscles. At other joints there are more than two muscles, which enables a greater variety of movement.

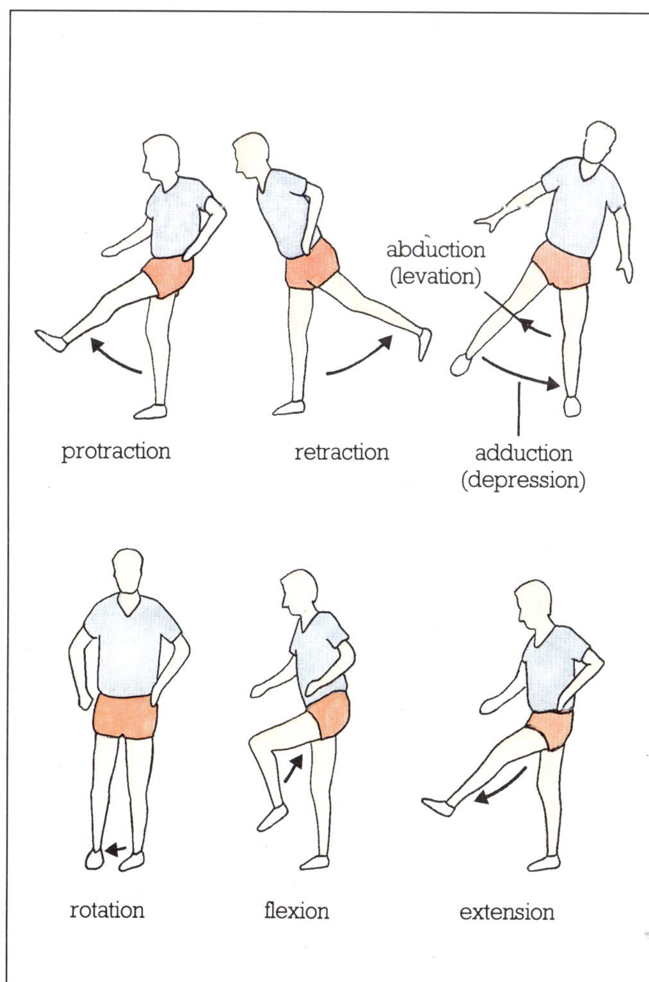

(Above) The actions produced by the muscles in the human leg.

(Top) The structure of a long bone (tibia).

Structure of skeletal muscle.

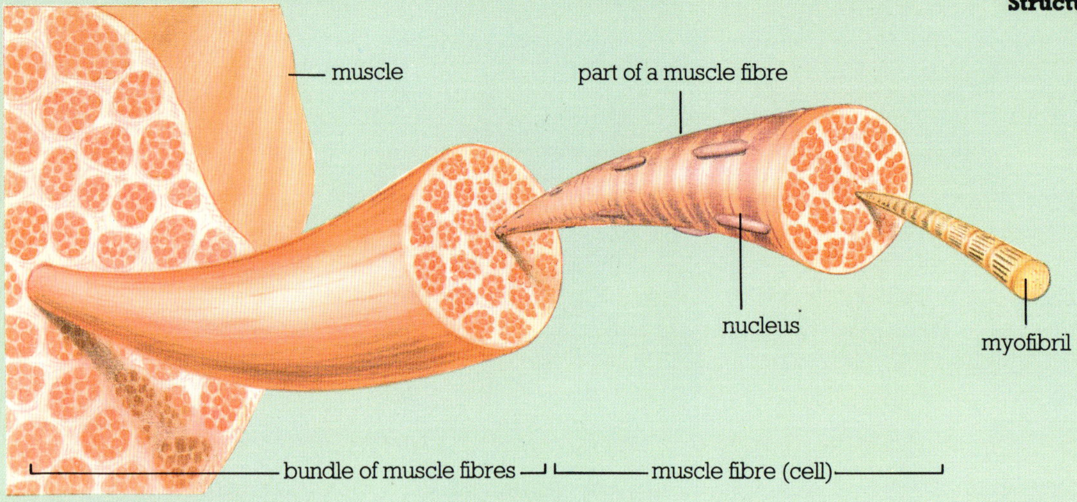

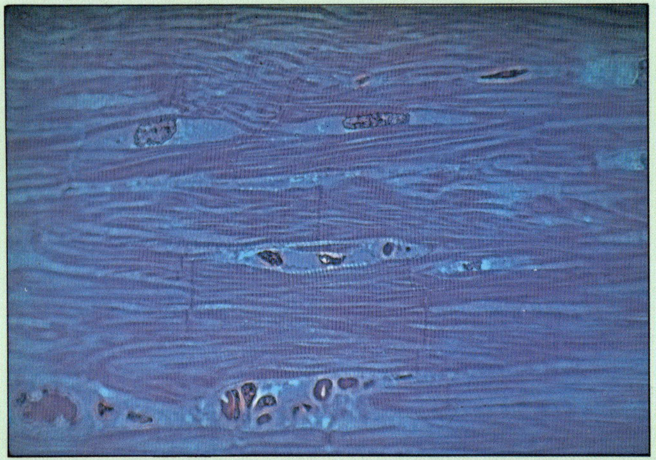

Cardiac muscle.

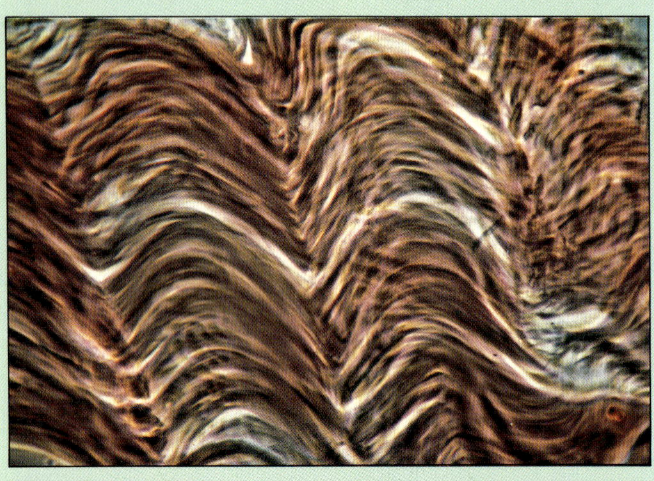

Smooth muscle.

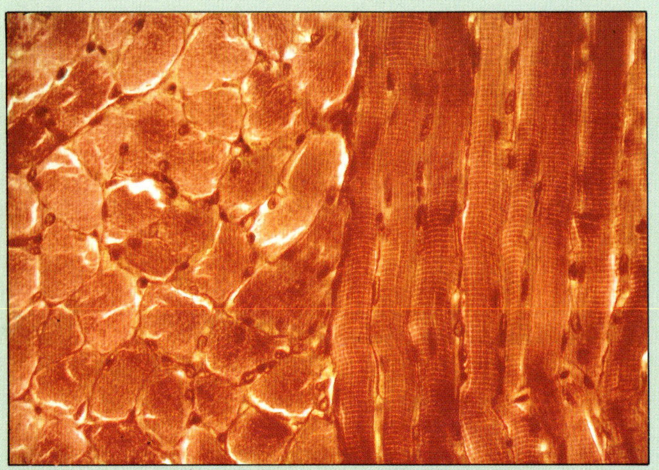

Skeletal muscle.

HOW MUSCLES WORK

There are three sorts of muscle. **Cardiac muscle** is only found in the heart, and is a very specialised type of muscle. **Smooth, or involuntary muscle** is found lining the bladder and in the tube of the digestive system. As is indicated by the name, we cannot consciously control these muscles. Food is moved through the digestive system by this type of muscle, and if the body is rejecting food, the reflexes of vomiting and diarrhoea make us aware how strong these muscles can be.

The third type of muscle is **striped (striated) or skeletal muscle**. This is voluntary muscle, and we control this in order to move.

Skeletal muscles are made up of thousands of muscle fibres. These fibres vary in length from 1mm to more than 40 cm. When a muscle contracts, the filaments in the fibres slide over each other resulting in a shortening of the fibres. The combined effect is to make the muscle shorter and fatter, rather like ripple shuffling a pack of playing cards.

There are two kinds of fibres found in skeletal muscles, slow-twitch fibres and fast-twitch fibres.

Slow-twitch fibres

Slow-twitch fibres contain a substance called myoglobin. Myoglobin stores oxygen and will give it up only if oxygen is in very short supply. This means that slow-twitch fibres are likely to have plenty of oxygen, from the haemoglobin in the blood supplying the muscle and the extra store from the myoglobin. Because of this, slow-twitch fibres can satisfy nearly all their energy needs from aerobic respiration. Myoglobin is a dark red pigment which makes the slow-twitch fibres red. These fibres are comparatively slow to contract, but fatigue very slowly.

Fast-twitch fibres

Fast-twitch fibres are a pale colour. They differ from slow-twitch fibres because they have large stores of glycogen. The fibres depend on anaerobic respiration to supply their energy, so they can only work for a short length of time before exhausting their glycogen reserves and becoming fatigued. These fibres are very fast and powerful when they contract.

Everyone has both slow-twitch and fast-twitch fibres in their skeletal muscles. The relative amounts of the two types differs from person to person. Athletes who participate in power sports, which involve a large amount of effort for a short period of time (for example sprinters, jumpers and weight lifters), tend to have a larger proportion of

TYPE OF ATHLETE	FAST-TWITCH FIBRES	SLOW-TWITCH FIBRES
Sprinter	63%	37%
Jumper	63%	37%
Weight lifter	55%	45%
1500 m swimmer	26%	74%
Marathon runner	18%	82%

fast-twitch fibres. Athletes who participate in sports which require a more sustained effort over a long length of time (for example long-distance runners and cyclists) have a larger percentage of slow-twitch fibres.

The proportions of fast-twitch to slow-twitch fibres can be established by means of a **muscle biopsy**, where a small piece of muscle tissue is removed and examined microscopically. It is thought extremely unlikely that even intensive training favouring the use of one type of fibre will change the relative proportions of the two types, although carefully designed training can improve the performance of one type or another.

There is a line of thought that all would-be athletes should undergo a muscle biopsy to decide which type of sport they would be most likely to succeed in!

Different sports require different clothing.

PREPARING FOR EXERCISE

Before undertaking any exercise, make sure that you have considered the following points.

- The exercise is appropriate to your level of fitness
- You are wearing sensible clothing and footwear
- There is enough time to warm up for the exercise properly
- There is enough time to cool down, shower and change
- If you have had any serious illnesses, you have taken medical advice before you undertake anything strenuous. Older people should always follow this advice.

Appropriate exercise

It is important that the exercise which you choose to do is appropriate. If you have not undertaken any exercise for a considerable length of time, then you would be foolish to attempt to play one hour of squash against a very fit opponent. In the same way, you should not go to an advanced aerobics class if you have never been to aerobics before.

This also applies to sports with a high skill factor. It is very easy to injure yourself if your techniques and skills aren't the same as your team members or opponents. This is why there are systems of handicapping for many sports, or different divisions for different abilities. There are also different categories in major competitions for the disabled, so that everyone competes at a comparable level. There are also different categories in the World Transplant Games, which are open to competitors who have undergone organ transplants.

If you are starting to exercise, start with something gentle, and build up over a period of time.

Clothing and footwear

Clothing and footwear should be appropriate to the particular type of exercise. All clothing should be washable, and washed regularly. It should be loose enough so that it doesn't restrict movement, but not so loose that it gets in the way of the exercise. It is important to be warm enough during exercise, and also directly after finishing exercise.

Footwear is also important. Shoes should support and protect your feet and be of the right size and type for the sport you are doing.

It is vital for anyone taking part in sport to wear suitable shoes. When all the published information about sports shoes was considered together, several points to consider when choosing footwear became clear. How firmly is the foot fixed, how much friction is there between the sole and the surface, how much torque is there, how many studs (cleats) on the shoe and how long are the studs? These are all important things to think about.

Torque is the twisting mechanism which lets limbs move freely and is especially relevant in sports such as netball and tennis, where there is sideways movement. Too much torque can result in injury and too little in restriction of movement. The amount of torque allowed by shoes depends partly on the depth of the studs; if they are too long, the shoes get fixed and sideways movement is dangerous. On the other hand, if there are no studs, the shoes will not give any friction, particularly on artificial surfaces.

The international athlete Steve Cram has said that safe shoes should have six characteristics – they should grip the foot properly, absorb shock, give support and be affordable, of good quality and stylish.

Warming up
There are several reasons why you should warm up properly before exercise.

1. It reduces the risk of injury during exercise.
2. It enables you to gain maximum benefit and enjoyment from the exercise.
3. It ensures that your performance is at its best from the start of the exercise.
4. It gives you time to think and mentally prepare for your exercise.

The time needed for a good warm-up depends on what type of exercise you are about to undertake and the level at which you are approaching it. Top class athletes entering an important competition will need at least thirty minutes of programmed warm-up if they are to perform well. A professional warm-up like this will end up with activities of the same strenuous level as the exercise about to be undertaken. Other less strenuous types of exercise may require as little as five minutes warming up. Some forms of exercise like aerobics actually build a warm-up into the session.

A warm-up should do three things: warm the body, increase mobility and stretch and gradually work all the muscles which you are going to use so that they have been used to their maximum by the end of the warm-up period.

Warming the body is achieved by increasing the blood flow to the muscles, thus increasing the amount of oxygen available to the muscles and preparing them for exercise.

Increasing mobility and movement of all the joints is important. This is best achieved by introducing gradual movement at the relevant joint, and then increasing the amount of movement. This loosens the joints and can also get rid of stiffness.

Stretching is important to reduce the risk of straining, pulling or tearing muscles. By slowly and gently stretching, and then, when warmer, increasing the stretch, the muscles will be well prepared for the exercise which is to follow.

It is very important that the warm-up should be progressive. Its purpose is to avoid injury, not to cause it. Many injuries are caused by people trying to overstretch muscles. If any stretching hurts, don't do it.

By the time this hurdler is positioned on the starting blocks he will have completed an extensive warm-up to prevent his muscles tearing when he launches into the race.

Cooling down
If possible, allow for a cooling down period after vigorous exercise. Walking or gently jogging around helps to clear any build up of lactic acid by keeping up the increased blood flow to the muscles. Gentle stretching can avoid stiffness and muscle damage. Whilst cooling down, it is important not to get too cold, so it is advisable to have extra clothing available. Cooling down should take at least ten minutes.

After all but the most gentle exercise, it is important to shower and change into fresh clothing. Showering cleans away the stale sweat which can irritate the skin, making it itch. Stale sweat also encourages bacterial growth which produces body odour (BO). Clothing used for exercise should be regularly washed for the same reasons.

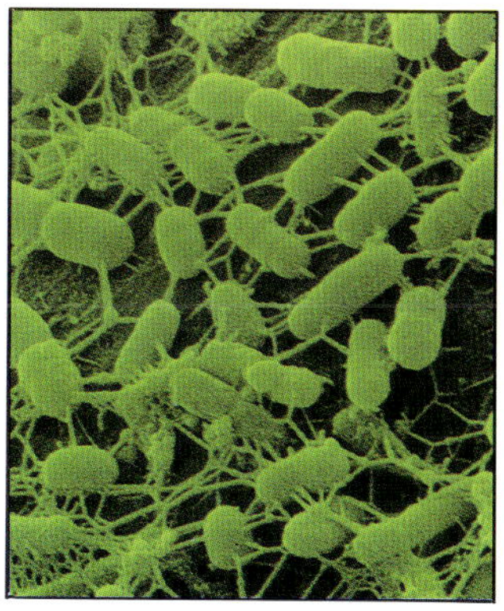

A scanning electron micrograph showing the bacteria present in a sample of dirty clothing.

It is also important to replace any water lost due to sweating. Despite extravagant claims from some drinks manufacturers, water rehydrates our bodies quicker than other drinks. It is essential to replace the salt lost during sweating by making sure extra is eaten.

Stretching exercises are a crucial part of a good warm-up programme.

WHAT HAPPENS TO OUR BODIES WHEN WE EXERCISE?

When we exercise, we use energy. Only about 25% of this energy is actually used by the muscle, the rest is given out as heat. Our body temperature will rise and, as a result, we start to sweat. As the sweat evaporates off our skins, heat is removed.

As mentioned previously (p. 20), we get our energy from ATP breaking down into ADP. The ATP present in the body would only fuel 3 to 5 seconds of exercise. ATP is not stored, so for exercise lasting longer than this energy must be obtained from other sources. A chemical called phosphocreatine is broken down and the energy released from this converts ADP back to ATP. With this supply, the body would be able to undertake about 10–15 seconds of strenuous exercise.

The energy which enables us to exercise for longer lengths of time comes from our food reserves. When ATP and phosphocreatine supplies have been used, the glucose in our blood will be used to resynthesise ATP by aerobic respiration. This respiration requires oxygen, so we will breathe more rapidly to ensure that we take in enough oxygen. The larger the muscle group used, the more energy it needs, so the higher the rate of breathing.

The energy produced will be used to make ATP. As the glucose in the blood is used up, the carbohydrate store of glycogen is converted into glucose to be used as a respiratory fuel.

We have a store of about 500g of glycogen, three-quarters of which is stored in the muscles, and the remaining quarter in the liver. If the level of exercise is constant and the energy requirement is not more than the energy produced by respiration, the glycogen store will last for about ninety minutes. After this, fat is broken down to produce the energy to make ATP.

Athletes cannot exercise continuously for very long periods even if they have ample fat supplies. Fat takes time to break down so it is less immediate. The power output of an athlete relying on fat as a fuel can be half that of an athlete using glycogen. Our brains also require glucose, and, if we exhaust our glycogen supplies, the brain will be deprived. This is why during very punishing events like the Iron Man triathlons where the competition lasts for many hours, athletes will take in glucose drinks at points along the way.

Many athletes believe that taking glucose or fructose before a race can help them. The disadvantage of glucose is that, soon afterwards, the blood level may fall through the action of insulin released. Fructose, which has been favoured by swimmers, is better in this respect because it doesn't release insulin. Many games players favour a diet rich in complex carbohydrates for 1-2 days before a big event to build up reserves of glycogen and fat, in the blood, for energy.

If we push our exertion over the level where we can rely on aerobic respiration, we start to produce energy anaerobically from glycogen.

We can only do this for a relatively short time, as the lactic acid quickly builds up and this makes our muscles feel like jelly. The pH of the muscle is altered and the enzymes responsible for our chemical reactions will not be able to work unless or until they switch over to using fatty acids for fuel. Training probably helps this process. Lactic acid build-up also causes pain, but pain is one of our body's natural defence mechanisms which tells us when to stop.

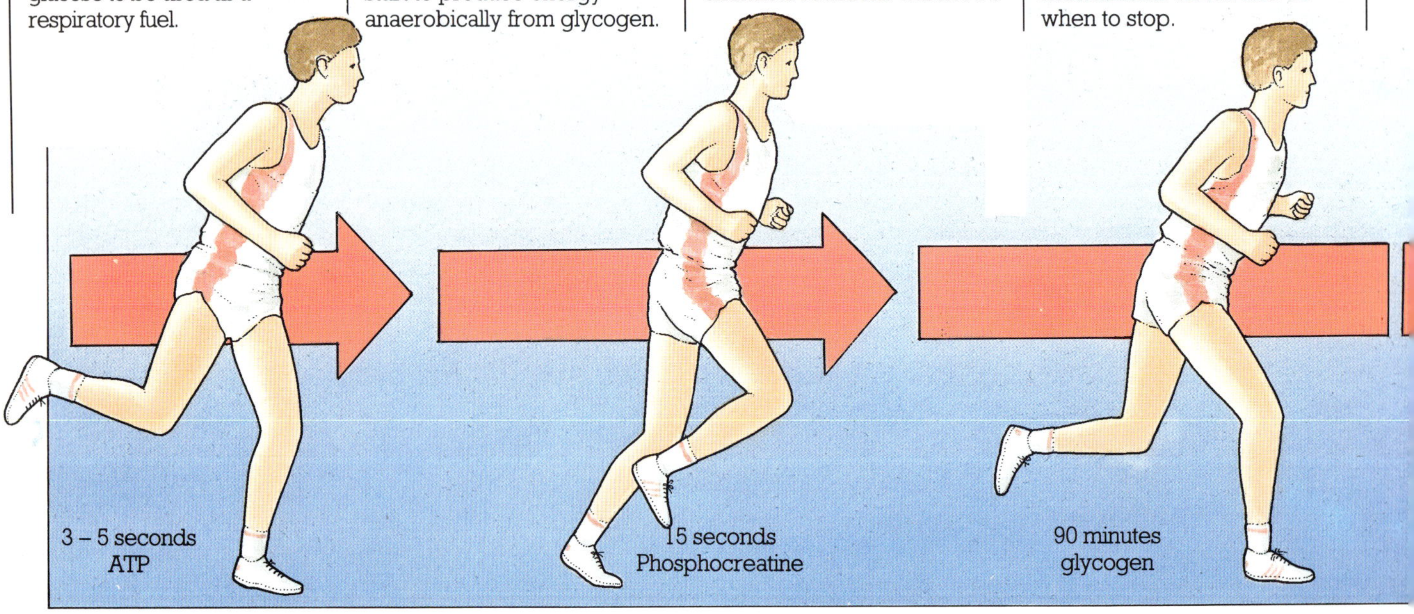

Other body changes during exercise

Heartbeat increases by as much as three to four fold (from 60 to about 180 beats/min)

The amount of blood pumped per beat goes up by three times

Breathing rate increases to three times the resting rate

Breathing becomes deeper

Blood is diverted from digestive system and urinogenital system to skeletal muscles

Body temperature rises by as much as 5°C

Water content drops because of sweating

Long-term consequences of aerobic exercise

If you exercise regularly, then your body adapts so that it is more efficient for exercise.

Your circulatory (blood) system becomes more efficient. Your resting heartbeat will go down, by perhaps as many as twenty beats per minute. Very fit athletes can have a resting rate of 35 beats per minute. The heart pumps more blood per beat, so the amount of blood at rest will be the same as that of a less fit person with a higher resting rate. This means that when exercise is undertaken, the amount of blood pumped per minute will be considerably more as the maximum heart beat will remain at about 180–200 beats/min. The number of capillaries in the muscles also increases, which means that there is a bigger supply of oxygen and glucose and fatty acids to the muscles. The level of cholesterol in the blood generally falls.

Skeletal muscles increase in size. This is because the muscle fibres increase in size. Some fibres occasionally split down the middle to form new fibres. The number of muscle cells cannot actually increase. There is an increase in the number of mitochondria, important cell organelles involved with energy production. Available amounts of ATP, phosphocreatine, glycogen and fat in the muscles increase.

How healthy is exercise?

There is no doubt that appropriate exercise is good for you. Often it can give you a sense of well-being and self-confidence, and its physical effects on the body are beneficial to good health.

The physical skills which you use during exercise improve. Balance, co-ordination, strength and flexibility improve. Ligaments, tendons and bones are strengthened. Reaction times often speed up.

Circulation improves. This can lead to an improvement in skin condition and tone. Digestion often improves and there may well be a weight loss in people who are overweight.

Blood pressure often decreases and there is some evidence that as the blood cholesterol level falls, atherosclerosis (thickening of the arteries) is slowed down, and in some cases reversed. This means that there is less likelihood of heart attacks.

People who exercise regularly find that they feel less tired. Fatigue takes longer to set in and the quality of sleep is better.

Note: All these effects are beneficial, but exercise, like most things, if carried out in excess can be harmful. Over-training in any sport can be harmful, especially in young athletes in whom it can lead to chronic tissue injury.

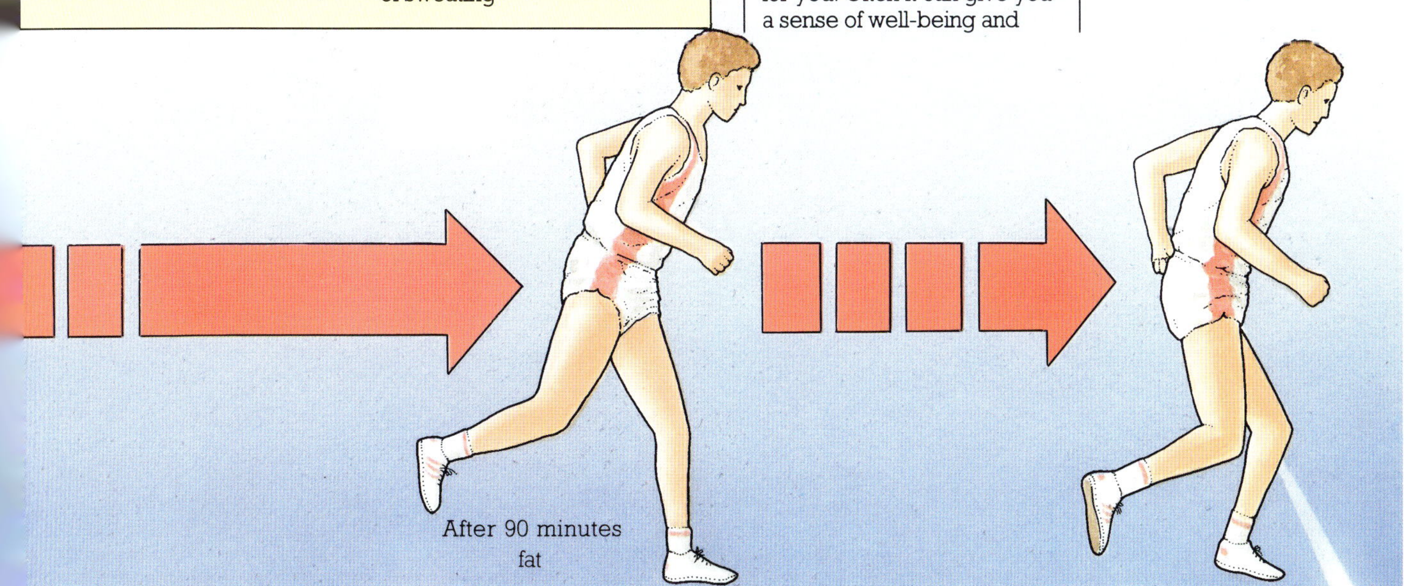

5: FEELING HEALTHY & FIT

It is no good exercising and being careful about what we eat, if we don't feel good about ourselves. Many people think that we have no control over how we feel. We may not have as much control over it as we have over some physical factors, but we can work at improving our mental health. Having a positive self image and looking critically at our lifestyle with a view to avoiding stress can help.

How you feel about yourself is very closely related to how you feel physically. If you are ill, you are often miserable, but once you get better your outlook on life can brighten considerably. It has been shown that people who are physically fit tend to be more confident and outgoing. They have a more relaxed attitude to life and have a positive self image. There is also some evidence that people who are in good shape mentally tend to get fewer illnesses. These aspects of health are very closely linked. People who are HIV positive and those with AIDS have shown increased antibody production after regular exercise.

SELF IMAGE
It is important to feel good about yourself. This means thinking about what you like about yourself, and not putting yourself down. It is not a good idea to compare your size and looks critically with those of a fashion model, your fitness with a world class athlete or your mental ability with Einstein! What is important is that you look for and recognise your good points and, if you do identify points that you are not happy with, you work on changing them.

It is also important to realise that different types of people like different characteristics. If you are worried about being too quiet, then remember that many people like quiet friends. We all have something to offer.

EXTERNAL PRESSURES
Your lifestyle, that is what you do and your attitude to health and fitness, is likely to be subjected to different pressures. Some of these come from you. Your anxieties about yourself and your ability, your confidence, your personality and your motivation will affect the way you behave. External or outside pressures include media pressure, peer pressure (pressure from friends and others of your age), parental pressure and pressure from other adults like teachers or coaches.

The pressure of the media affects many aspects of your lifestyle. Magazines and television try to influence how you dress, what sort of music you listen to and what sort of activities you should be involved in. This is not necessarily harmful – tennis clubs throughout the country report an upsurge in membership in the weeks following the Wimbledon Tennis championships.

Normal adults have been shown to benefit psychologically from regular, moderate physical exercise. After a 10-week period, people who had exercised regularly three times each week had reduced tension and anxiety levels and had improved their ability to think clearly and to cope with stress.

The pressure to conform and be the same as everyone else can be immense. It can lead to nervous disorders.

Weight concerns are established in most girls by the time they are 14 years old. Many are weight conscious by the time they are eleven.

There are numerous studies of young people to try to find out what makes some anorexic and some bulimic, while others are not, even though they are all interested in their weights and appearances. Ballet dancers have to be light and slim; but, although they are more likely than other adolescents to diet, they seem less likely to suffer from eating disorders. The same has been found to be true of jockeys; they stick to diets for long periods, so that they are light enough to race, but are not likely to suffer from bulimic or anorexic episodes.

ANOREXIA NERVOSA AND BULIMIA

Anorexia nervosa and bulimia are two nervous diseases which affect eating patterns. The most common age group of people affected by these diseases are teenagers and young adults between 15 and 25. It was estimated that 95% of those affected are female, although recent statistics show that the number of boys suffering from anorexia is on the increase.

Both diseases often start with the affected person getting over anxious about their weight. This is common. In a survey of over 9000 adults in England and Wales (the *Health and Lifestyle* survey), it was reported that 40% of adult women of normal weight considered themselves too heavy.

(Top) Magazines try to influence how we look, what clothes we wear and what our homes should look like.

(Bottom) Ballet dancers are usually very slender but they rarely suffer from eating disorders.

Anorexics get obsessive about their weight, and eat less and less. They often hide this fact from their family and friends and appear to be extremely interested in food; they often claim to be hungry. Even when anorexics are dangerously underweight, they will still perceive themselves to be fat. Anorexics need careful counselling and medical help so that they can recover. If their weight loss has been very high, there is the possibility that permanent damage has been done to their health. In girls, periods will stop, and, in extreme cases, heart failure due to a weakening of the heart muscles can occur.

Bulimics are also obsessed with food. They tend to 'binge' – eating far more than normal, then make themselves sick so that they vomit up all the food before it is digested. They also take laxatives and diuretics. Laxatives make them go to the toilet more often to get rid of solid waste, and diuretics stop the kidney reabsorbing water, so the person urinates more frequently.

Bulimics usually stay at their normal body weight, but the continuous overeating and vomiting damages the digestive system. In extreme cases of binging, stomachs have been known to rupture. Teeth can be damaged by the acid brought up from the stomach during vomiting. Bulimics are not as secretive as anorexics and rarely hide their condition. With help, most bulimics can be cured.

Bulimics and anorexics are characterised by their poor self image. They are often depressed, and can feel suicidal. Friends and families can help by encouraging sufferers to feel good about themselves.

STRESS

We feel stressed when we are put under pressure. This can be for many different reasons. A small amount of stress can often improve our performance or, at worse, make us feel a little tense. As stress builds up, we may start to get physical symptoms and if we are put under serious stress, it can have a very harmful effect on our health.

PHYSICAL SIGNS OF STRESS	MENTAL SIGNS OF STRESS
Headaches	Irritability
Chest pains	Bad temper
High blood pressure	Depression
Insomnia	Inability to concentrate
Eczema	Overreacting to problems
Asthma	Inability to relax
Palpitations	Intolerance of noise
Tiredness	Impulsive behaviour
Dandruff	Feeling panicky

Coping with stress – some ways out

A good way of coping with stress is to reduce the levels by avoiding stressful situations. If you can easily identify the circumstances in which you feel stressed, then you can take avoiding action. It is stressful having to explain to your teacher why your exam coursework isn't finished. You may find it easier if you organise yourself to meet deadlines for homework. List-making and work timetables can help. Exams can be less stressful if you have prepared properly for them. Obviously, there will be some causes of stress that are out of your control.

If you have an active lifestyle you should be able to cope with life's stresses and strains. Research has shown that exercise relaxes people more than smoking or drinking.

Another strategy is to reduce the effects of stress. Rest and relaxation are important. Sometimes, giving yourself time on your own away from distractions can be enough. Relaxation techniques can also help. One which is used by many people on their own involves thinking about different muscles, tensing them, then letting them completely relax. Yoga can also be beneficial.

The main muscle groups to think of are:
shin and calf
thigh and buttock
back and abdominal
chest
shoulder and arm
face and neck.

After you have worked through the muscles, think about breathing slowly and deeply. This exercise will only work if you concentrate on what you are doing and try not to think about anything else. As the object of this exercise is to relax, it is sensible to do it when you have time to get the maximum benefit, just before you go to sleep for example.

The major muscle groups in the human body.

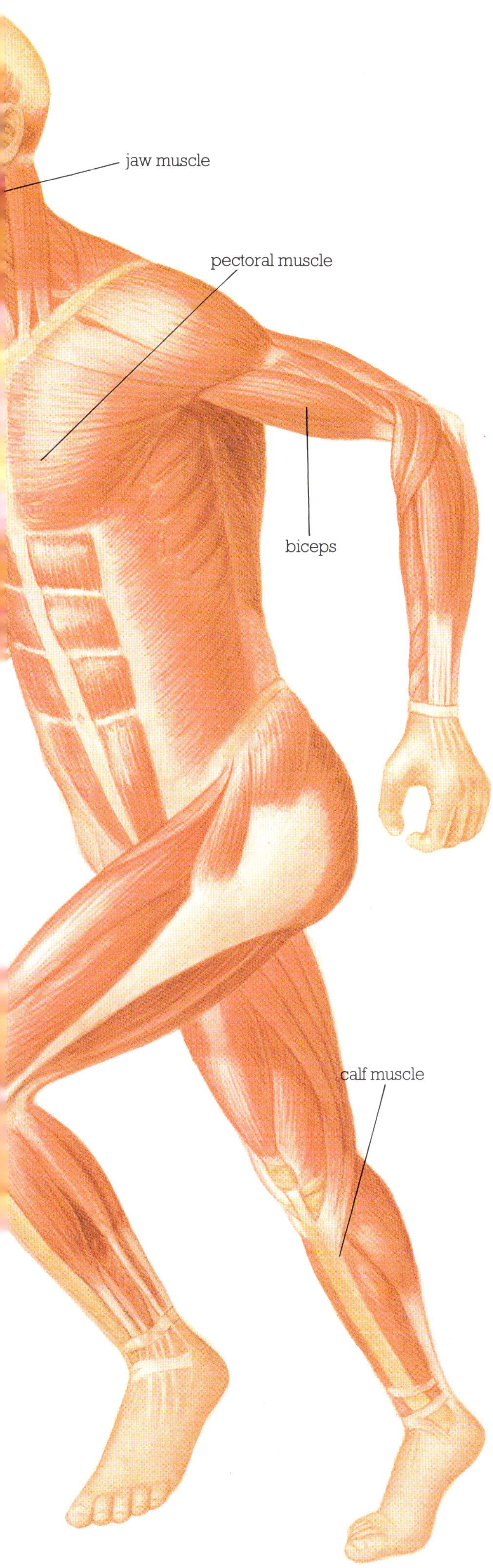

Some cases of stress-induced insomnia can be relieved by doing something energetic. Often when you are mentally tired, you feel lethargic and too tired to take any exercise. Research has shown that a moderate amount of exercise can make you feel more alert and motivated for a short period of time and, when you go to bed, because you are physically as well as mentally tired, you can sleep soundly. Exercise has also been shown to help some people suffering from mental disorders, for example from depression and schizophrenia.

WAYS TO IMPROVE YOUR MENTAL HEALTH
If you decide to examine your lifestyle, your physical health and your self image critically, you may teel that you want to improve aspects of what you see. It is important to take the following points into consideration.

1. Motivation. Why am I wanting to change? Is it for the right reasons?

If a change is to be effected you must want to do it. As much of the motivation must come from you, you must be sure about why you are making the change.

2. Setting goals. Am I being realistic? Will I have any success?

If you set goals which are unrealistic, you will be unable to meet them and this could worsen your situation because you will feel less worthy. For example, it is unrealistic to run a marathon after only one month's training, expect a complete personality change overnight or expect to lose 5 kg of weight in a week. Set goals that are within your reach, and promise yourself a reward if you succeed.

3. Help. Do I need any help or support in achieving my goal?

Some changes are easier to do if you have help. Giving up smoking is easier if you are surrounded by supportive friends. Taking up exercise is easier if someone is helping you or joining in.

When things go wrong
Sometimes, it is not possible to improve your mental health without help. Some people feel so miserable and depressed that they turn to unprescribed drugs. Many resort to alcohol. Alcohol is a depressant, so, if you are miserable, being drunk will make you worse. It seems to exaggerate all moods, so if you tend to be violent when you are upset, it is likely to make you provoke a fight. This, together with the fact that excessive amounts of alcohol are regarded by the body as a poison and can make you feel very ill the following day, should tell you that alcohol will not solve any problems.

Other drugs, like many of the illegal, highly addictive drugs may make you feel better, but only for a very short time. The long-term effects are that immediately following the 'high', you would experience a 'low' which is likely to be lower than the state which you were in before. If you continue to take the drug, the highs cease to be so strong and you end up taking the drugs just to feel normal. If you do not have the drug, you not only feel depressed, you will also have physical withdrawal symptoms which make you feel very ill indeed.

It is best to seek medical help if you feel you can't cope. A doctor may suggest counselling, where someone will listen to your problems and try to help. He or she may prescribe mild tranquillisers or sleeping tablets if you are really not coping. These must be regarded as a temporary solution while you try to improve your situation. Even prescribed drugs can be addictive, and can lead to long-term dependence, which will add to your problems.

Another addiction is one of exercise dependence. Very occasionally, athletes become addicted to training. One theory is that you produce natural chemicals when you push yourself in training which give you a natural 'high' and you become addicted to this. People who are exercise dependent continue to train even when injured and keep to unrealistically intensive training programmes. They become over-tired, and show changes in personality. This is very rare, and most people easily overcome this problem.

6: HOW FIT ARE YOU?

It is often difficult to gauge how effective any change in lifestyle is. If you have been attempting to become more physically healthy, it is only by carefully monitoring your fitness and regularly retesting yourself that you can find out how successful any exercise or diet regime is.

If you are not obviously overweight or underweight, if you are satisfied with your diet and lifestyle, and are showing none of the physical signs of stress, then it is likely that you are relatively healthy. However, to work out just how fit you are, and if you can maintain or improve this, you have to find a way of measuring fitness.

One way of assessing how physically fit you are is by looking at your weight compared with your height.

There are many charts available, and it is easy to see if you fall within the recommended limits. Whilst it is important to realise that if you are very overweight your health will improve if you lose weight, it is also important to be realistic about a target weight, and not expect to lose, for example, half your body weight.

It is not healthy to be very underweight either, although this often appears to be more acceptable and to look better.

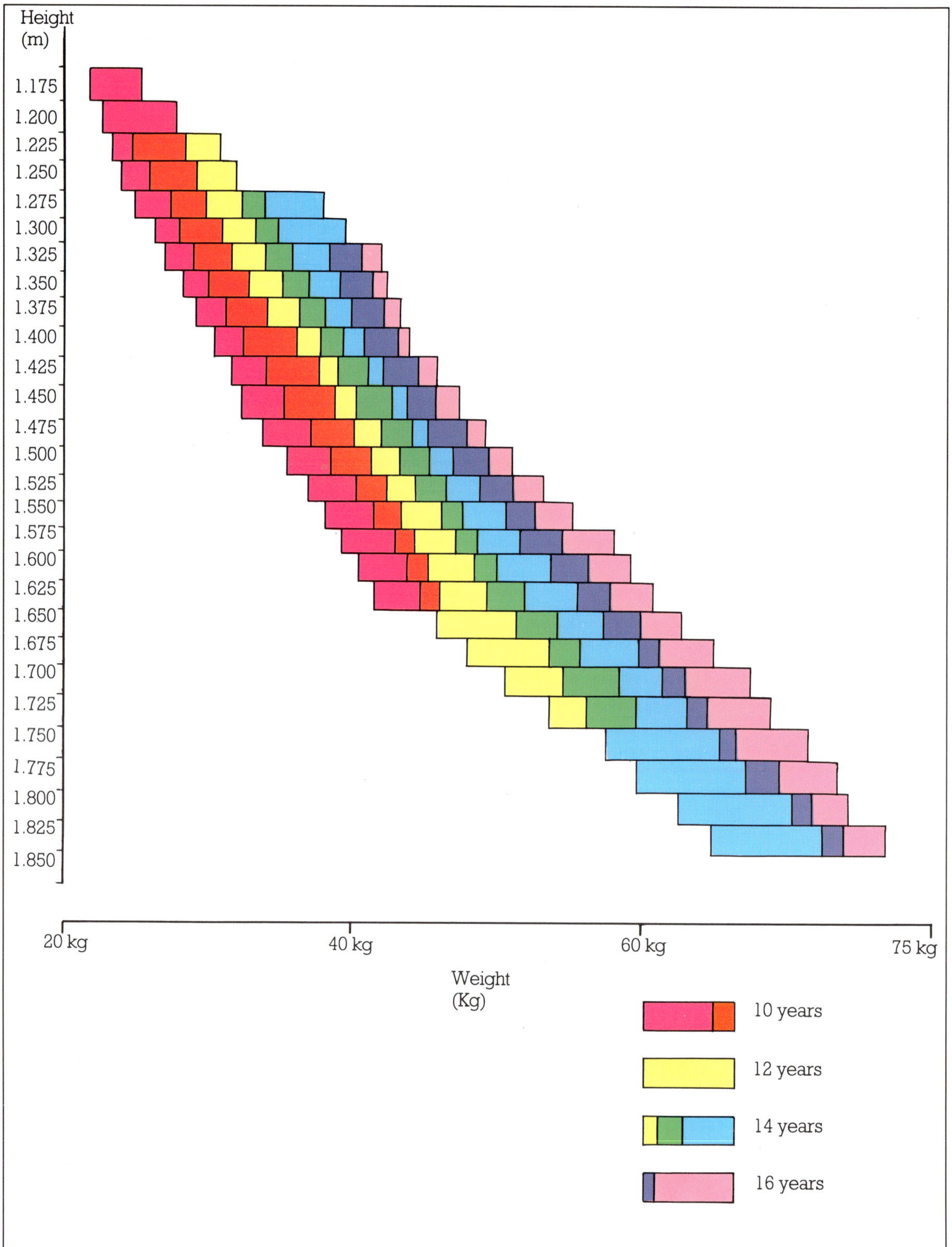

An example of a height/weight chart.

It is a fact that some people have larger frames than others, and it is unrealistic for them to expect, even with strict dieting and plenty of exercise, that they will attain fashion model type proportions. Everyone has a different body shape, and there is nothing that you can do to alter that basic shape. You have inherited this, along with your other characteristics, from your parents. Half the coding information is from your mother and half from your father.

Body shapes have been loosely categorised into three main types – ectomorphs, mesomorphs and endomorphs. Many characteristics and character traits have been attributed to these different shapes. It is rare that people are pure mesomorphs, endomorphs or ectomorphs. Most people would recognise bits of each in themselves.

Obviously, deciding which weight you should be will also depend on which body type you appear to have. If you are in any doubt as to whether you are over or underweight, go to see your doctor.

MEASURING FITNESS

Resting heart rate

You can get an indication of how physically fit you are by working out your resting heart rate. Taking your pulse gives you your heart rate. There are two places where pulses are most commonly taken. The first, the radial pulse, is taken by pressing the finger tips of one hand against the radial artery in the other wrist. The other convenient place to take your pulse is the neck, where you feel the pulse in the carotid artery. When you have found your pulse in either place, count the number of beats in thirty seconds and then double it to give you the number of heart beats per minute. The fitter you are, the lower your resting heart rate and the quicker your recovery rate after exercise.

It is important that you are as rested as possible before taking your pulse. Ideally it should be several hours after you have eaten. The best time is probably just after you wake up naturally – not when you're recovering from the effects of your alarm clock!

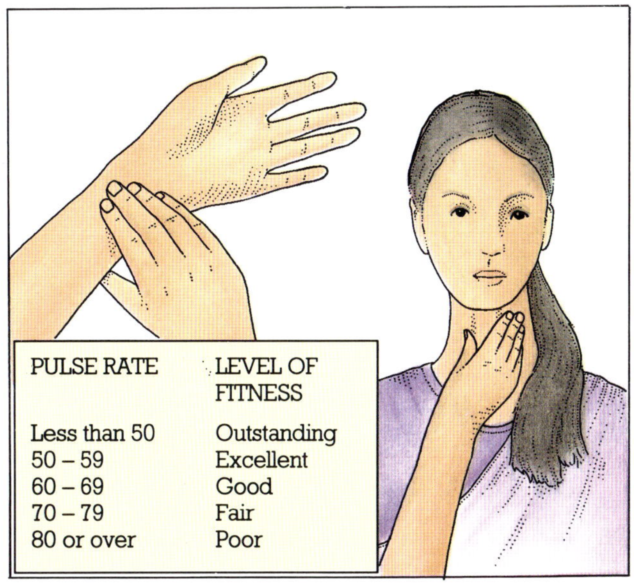

PULSE RATE	LEVEL OF FITNESS
Less than 50	Outstanding
50 – 59	Excellent
60 – 69	Good
70 – 79	Fair
80 or over	Poor

The pulse can be taken by feeling an accessible artery in the wrist or in the neck.

(It is also worth remembering the effect on your heart of drugs like caffeine (found in coffee, cola drinks and tea) when you measure resting rate. The nicotine in cigarettes speeds up the heart rate also.)

This method of measuring your aerobic fitness has several advantages. It is quick to do and requires no more specialised equipment than a watch with a second hand. It has several drawbacks. It isn't very sensitive. Many other factors affect your heart rate. There are even a few people who have naturally low pulse rates even when they are very unfit, and others who are very fit but have a higher than average resting rate.

Ectomorphs –
tall for their weight, less fitted to robust activities.

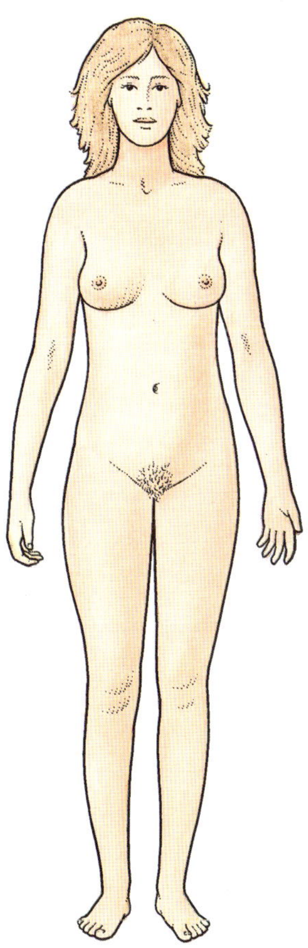

Mesomorphs –
average build, robust and athletic.

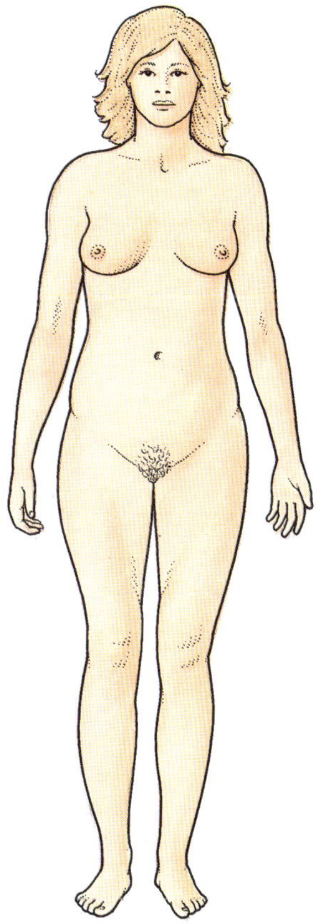

Endomorphs –
tend to be overweight, and therefore less suited to mobile activities.

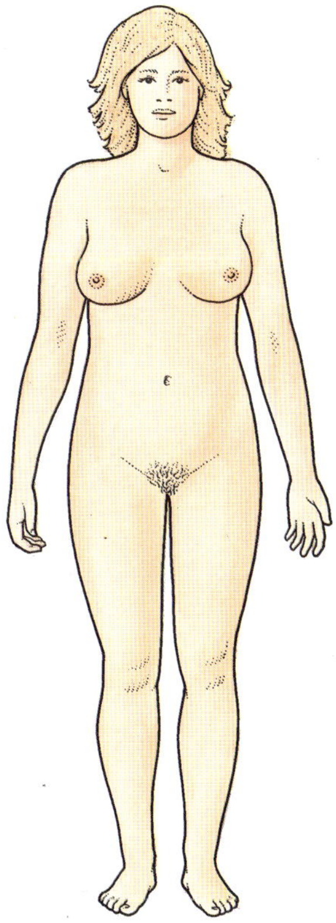

Step-up test
By taking your pulse rate after a set amount of exercise, you can calculate where you are on a fitness index. The amount of work you do as part of this test has been carefully calculated, so it is essential that you use apparatus of the correct height.

The step-up test consists of the subject stepping on and off a bench or chair at a rating of thirty complete steps per minute – stepping up and down – for five minutes.

The height of step used varies with the age and sex of the subject.

After the subjects have completed the five minutes (or as many as they can), they should sit down and rest for one minute. They should then take their pulse for 30 seconds. Using the following formula, it will be possible to calculate a fitness index (FI).

$$FI = \frac{(\text{duration of test in seconds}) \times 100}{(\text{pulse count for 30 seconds}) \times 5.5}$$

After working out the fitness index, they can work out how fit they are from the table on this page.

AGE AND SEX OF SUBJECT	HEIGHT OF STEP
Female aged 14 – 17	16 in
Female aged 18 and over	18 in
Male aged 14 – 15	16 in
Male aged 16 – 17	18 in
Male aged 18 and over	20 in

FITNESS INDEX	AEROBIC FITNESS
180 or over	Superb
160 – 179	Excellent
140 – 159	Very good
120 – 139	Good
100 – 119	Creditable
80 – 99	Reasonable

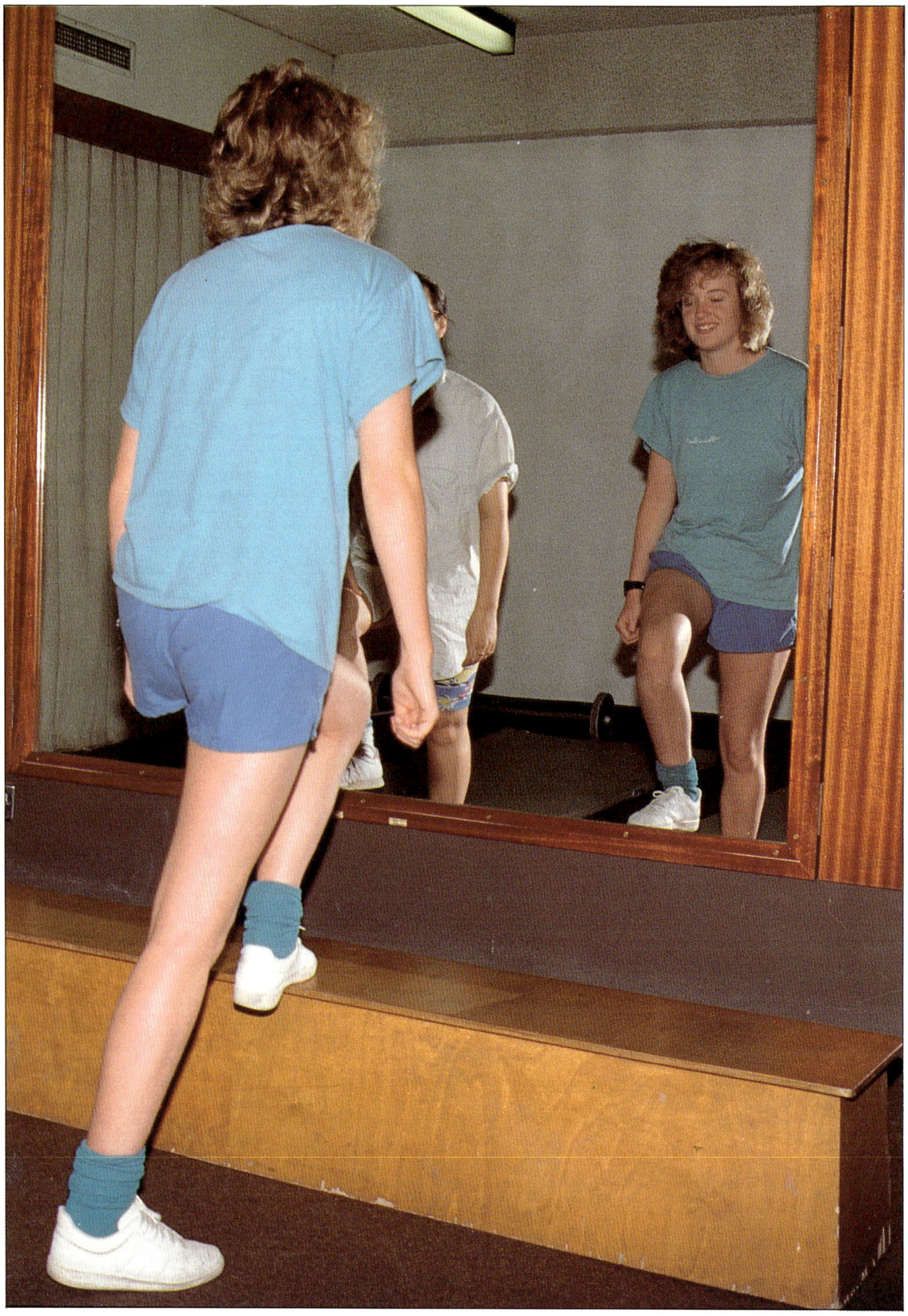

Running as a measure of fitness
A simple way of getting a measure of how fit you are is to time how long it takes you to run a certain distance, one mile for example. It is important that you measure the distance accurately. Alternatively, you can see what distance you manage to run in seven minutes.

The 10 x 5 metre sprint test is useful in assessing speed over the 5-metre track and in giving a measure of co-ordination and agility.

A simple fitness battery can be used as a basis for deriving and monitoring training schedules for high level sports performers, as well as for measuring the development of skill in normally active school children.

Both these methods can be used even if at first you are unable to run 1 mile or keep going for seven minutes. Attempt to complete the distance or time by a combination of jogging, running and walking. If you train by attempting this distance four times a week for about six weeks, you should be able to go the distance or time quite easily.

With running tests, it is important that you wear suitable, good quality running shoes and that you run on soft, even ground like grass, shale or cinder track. Road or pavement running should be avoided, because it can cause sore feet and jar the joints.

A step-up test.

Shuttle run

A shuttle run test requires a gym or an area which is over 20 metres in length and a prerecorded audio tape (available from the National Coaching Foundation). Lines or tapes at twenty metres apart should be marked. This tape is currently available from The National Coaching Foundation, 4 College Close, Beckett Park, Leeds, LS6 6EF.

This test starts with a spoken introduction, then a series of signals. The subject should run between the two lines so that each end is reached as the signal sounds. The test is progressive in that the signals become closer and closer together, requiring the subject to run more and more quickly. The test ends when the subject can no longer keep up the pace set by the signals. The number of successful shuttle runs gives an indication of fitness.

A shuttle run test in progress.

KEEPING WELL

Fitness and health are not all about exercise and training, they are also about keeping well. Sometimes, through no fault of your own, you catch an infectious disease, or are injured. If you are ill, it is important to be sensible. It is better to rest, to drink a lot of fluid and allow your body time to recover than to keep going, tiring yourself out and not recovering as quickly. It takes a lot of energy to fight infection, and, if you get very tired, secondary infections may result.

Being ill can cause a rise in body temperature. Because of this, it is very foolish to do any vigorous exercise if you have a temperature, as exercise alone can raise your temperature by up to 5°C even when you are healthy.

A large rise in temperature can be fatal.

It is also important to take notice of any symptoms of illness, and to act on them immediately. Symptoms can be an indication of something more serious going wrong so it is sensible to go to the doctor with any long-term symptom.

Of course, preventing disease is very important. Vaccination against common infectious diseases is sensible. Vaccinations work by giving you a harmless dose of either the disease-causing microbe or part of it, so that your body produces specialised antibodies to fight the microbe. This means that if any of the microbes invade your body at a later stage, it is well prepared and able to fight them before they make you ill.

Other ways of helping to ensure good health include eating sensibly and following sensible guidelines to avoid diseases, such as some cancers. The 'greenhouse effect' increases the importance of avoiding too much direct sunlight. In a recent campaign ten points were made in the effort to reduce cancer. Many of these guidelines also help to improve our health generally.

The 'Europe against cancer' ten point plan:

1. Do not start smoking. If you do smoke, give up immediately. The tar in smoke contains a carcinogen (cancer causing substance), so smoking increases the likelihood of cancer of the lung, mouth, oesophagus (food pipe) and bladder.

2. Drink alcohol in moderation. Drinking too much alcohol, as well as damaging your liver, can cause cancer of the larynx, mouth, oesophagus and liver.

3. Avoid being overweight. As well as putting your heart under more strain, if you are more than 20% overweight, you are increasing the likelihood of getting certain cancers associated with obesity.

4. Take care in the sun. Over-exposure to sun, especially when it is infrequent (a two-week holiday once a year, for instance), can cause skin cancer, particularly amongst fair skinned people.

5. Avoid exposure to known carcinogenic chemicals. Fortunately, most known carcinogenic substances have been banned from schools and places of work, and others are strictly controlled. Never disregard handling instructions for chemicals.

6. Cut down on fatty foods. Some people think that this may help to reduce the risk of breast and bowel cancer.

7. Eat more fibre. By eating plenty of fresh fruit and vegetables, wholegrain cereals and unrefined foods, you are less likely to get bowel cancer.

8. If your health suddenly changes or you have symptoms which last for more than two weeks, check with your doctor. You are unlikely to have cancer, but should be checked anyway.

9. Adult women should have a regular cervical smear test. This test involves taking a few cells from the cervix (neck of the womb). It is possible to detect any changes in the cells which may lead to cancer. This test should be carried out on all sexually active women every three to five years.

10. Adult women should check their breasts regularly. This is to detect any changes, for example lumps, dimples, puckering. This is often difficult as breast tissue is quite lumpy anyway. If there is any cause for worry, a doctor should be consulted.

Many of the above points will also help to prevent other diseases like heart disease and circulatory disorders. It is important to realise that you have some control over some of these.

7: EXERCISE FOR ALL

If you have measured your fitness and want to improve on it, you must decide how you want to proceed. Your body will need some form of exercise if you are to become fitter. Whether you exercise on your own, or with others is your choice. Incorporating exercise with an element of competition and some social contact by playing a team sport is a fun way of becoming fit. You should always introduce exercise to your routine at an appropriate level and build up to avoid injury.

WHY EXERCISE AT ALL?
If you look at a group of people, you may not be able to tell how many of them exercise regularly. It is possible to look fit even if you do not exercise at all. Your body will be as fit as it needs to be to carry out the exercise or work that you do. The more exercise you do, the more your body responds by getting fit. Chapter 4 lists the short-term and long-term advantages of aerobic exercise on the body (page 33).

People exercise for reasons other than just becoming more fit. Many adults exercise because they have a job which requires little physical effort and they like a complete change after work. Some exercise because it gives them a change of scene, or some fresh air. Others use exercise as a way of meeting new people and having a sociable time. Others enjoy competing against others or themselves in an organised sport.

HOW OFTEN TO EXERCISE

Exercise can improve different aspects of fitness. Aerobic fitness, and in particular aerobic endurance, will only improve with regular training with the heart working at a certain level. Specific exercises can improve speed and reaction time. Strength can be increased by a carefully planned weight-training programme. Suppleness and general mobility can be improved by stretching before and after each exercise session. This is important even in power sports to avoid injury.

Participating in different sports gives varying benefits. The table on the right lists several sports and physical activities and the effect which each type of exercise has on your stamina, suppleness and strength.

SPORT	STAMINA SCORE	SUPPLENESS SCORE	STRENGTH SCORE
Badminton	**	***	**
Canoeing	***	**	***
Climbing stairs	***	*	**
Cricket	*	**	*
Cycling (hard)	****	**	***
Dancing (ballroom)	*	***	*
Dancing (disco)	***	****	*
Digging (garden)	***	**	****
Football	***	***	***
Golf	*	**	*
Gymnastics	**	****	***
Hill walking	***	*	**
Housework (moderate)	*	**	*
Jogging	****	**	***
Judo	**	****	***
Mowing the lawn (by hand)	**	*	***
Rowing	****	**	****
Sailing	*	**	**
Squash	***	***	**
Swimming (hard)	****	****	****
Tennis	**	***	**
Walking briskly	**	*	*
Weight lifting	*	*	****
Yoga	*	****	*

* = No real benefit
** = Beneficial effect
*** = Very good effect
**** = Excellent effect

STAMINA BUILDING – AEROBIC EXERCISE

Aerobic exercise, if undertaken regularly and for a sufficient length of time, improves stamina. It is not enough to go out exercising if you do not push yourself so that your body is working hard. The easiest way to monitor how hard you are pushing yourself is to measure your heart rate.

Sport and exercise can be fun whatever age and shape we are. However, people over 35 or those who are very overweight should always consult their GP before doing any strenuous exercise.

Your maximum heart rate is approximately equal to 220 minus your age. This means that for a fourteen year old, your maximum heart rate will be 206. For a twenty year old it will be 200 and for a forty year old it will be 180. To improve your aerobic fitness, you should work at 70% of your maximum heart rate for at least twenty minutes, three times a week.

To make sure that the type of exercise you are doing is making you work at that level, you must monitor your heart rate during exercise. The best way is to undertake at least 5 minutes exercise, stop and take your pulse for ten seconds. By multiplying by 6, you can see if you have achieved your target.

AGE	MAXIMUM HEART RATE	70% OF MAXIMUM
15	205	145
20	200	140
30	190	135
40	180	125
50	170	120
60	160	110

STRENGTH
Most athletic performances will improve if there is an improvement in the strength of the participant. Improving strength means improving the general tone of the muscles and making them work harder than they normally do. This stimulates the muscles to adapt to cope with the extra strain. A carefully designed weights programme will achieve this. Obviously, if you try to lift weights that are too heavy, you may injure yourself badly. You should learn good techniques from a qualified instructor, start with weights that you can manage until you have mastered the techniques, and then progress to heavier and heavier weights.

If you are weight training to help you with a particular sport, it is best to ask your sports coach or an expert which exercises to use. This is to ensure that the right muscle groups are being worked on, and also that the action of the lift or exercise is appropriate to the sport.

Weight training two or three times a week will build up your strength. Session lengths should be between 30 minutes and an hour, but again, the length and frequency of the sessions should depend on the starting fitness of the individual. However, to keep any new-found strength, you need to continue to train once a week. If you have built up muscles from a previously weak state, they will quickly revert to their former state if you stop training altogether.

Weight training can involve using no more complicated equipment than your own body. By doing exercises that use your body weight, you can increase your strength. Examples of this type of exercise are sit-ups, press-ups, pull-ups on a bar, squat jumps.

Using a multi-gym is an accepted way of strength training. These expensive pieces of apparatus allow you to do specialised exercises. The weights are often lifted by pulleys and levers so that a comparatively light weight can feel more difficult! Multi-gyms are an ideal way of starting to weight train, as the techniques are quickly learned, and, if the stations are used properly, the risk of injury is often less than with other types of weights.

Free weights are the most difficult to learn as the risk of injury is high if you are inexperienced. Free weight exercises are very good at strengthening the major muscle groups.

SUPPLENESS/MOBILITY
The best way to increase suppleness is to do stretching exercises. The importance of stretching before any exercise has been mentioned on page 30. Stretching should, therefore, be incorporated into any aerobic or strength training sessions, or before competitive sport. Stretching reduces the risk of injury as well as improving the mobility of your joints.

SPEED AND REACTION TIME
Increasing speed is important for success in some sports, and, as speed training inevitably includes strength work and flexibility exercises, it can increase these aspects of fitness as well. Running speeds are improved by undertaking exercises involving sprinting for short periods, circuit training involving maximum effort, with rest intervals in between, and power/speed exercises.

HEALTHY COMPETITION?
If you exercise on your own, you can get bored. Circuit training can start to become tedious, and it is all too tempting to cut corners, miss out a few exercises, or, if you are running, either to take a short cut home or to start to walk. If you feel that this is happening, you must ask yourself why you are doing the exercise. If you find that you can't motivate yourself, set yourself targets and goals.

Try to compete against yourself, by going just a bit faster than last time, or a bit further. If you regularly test your fitness, by trying to improve your score you may regain your motivation.

Improving reaction time so that participants can react more quickly to, for example, a returning squash ball, a powerful tennis serve, or the starter's gun at the beginning of a race is an important area of training. This is usually improved by training. The psychological side of anticipation must also be considered. Balance and co-ordination also affect sports performance. The type of balance or coordination can be very specific. Often, these aspects will get better with practice.

If you still find it difficult, think seriously about persuading a friend to exercise with you, or exercise by competing in a sport. Look at your local facilities, choose a sport which appeals to you, and perhaps join a club. The element of competition is a strong motivating force. Again, it is important to compete against people of your own standard so you or they don't get discouraged and lose confidence.

8: THEORY INTO PRACTICE

This book has looked at different aspects of good health and how we can look after ourselves. Much of what affects our health is controllable by us. There are many ways in which the quality of our lives and the lives of people around us can be improved. Good health is important for us all.

The following are good aims to adopt if you want to improve your health. They are all controllable factors which contribute to good health. Some will not be easy to achieve on your own, as you may need the help and support of family and friends.

DIET

A good diet is a balanced diet. It should contain protein, carbohydrate, fibre, fat, vitamins, minerals and water. Most Western diets can be improved by:

- eating more complex carbohydrate and more fibre
- eating less fat, less salt and fewer simple carbohydrates
- eating regular meals and fewer 'fast food' snacks.

It is unhealthy to be either significantly underweight or overweight. The amount of food you eat should be controlled so that you maintain a sensible weight.

LOOKING AFTER YOUR LUNGS

We breathe so that we can get the oxygen which we need, and can get rid of carbon dioxide. Smoking damages our breathing system. Atmospheric pollution can also harm our lungs.

EXERCISE
Exercise is a way of improving our physical health. It should always be at the right level for our fitness. It is important to warm up and cool down properly when undertaking exercise. This helps us to avoid injury. There are many different ways of exercising. Taking part in sports can be a good, fun way of taking exercise.

MENTAL HEALTH
It is important to feel good about yourself and your good points. Don't dwell on the bad points. Try to set yourself realistic targets if you feel that you want to change. If you fail in reaching your target, set yourself a more realistic target for next time. Avoid stress by avoiding stressful situations or learning to relax to get rid of tension caused by stress.

ASSESSING FITNESS
Regular fitness testing can give you a measure of your aerobic fitness so that you can find out if you are improving through exercising.

CASE HISTORY

Look at the lifestyles of the people in the following case histories. Write down their good healthy habits – and any bad ones. Write down a list of realistic health related targets for each one.

How might you, as a friend, help?

Kate, aged 15.
Kate is studying for her GCSEs. She is behind in her work, and has two projects due in at the end of the week. She spends most evenings watching television with her friend who lives next door. She doesn't like to offend her friend by leaving early. Because of this, she works late at night, often until two or three o' clock in the morning. and is tired all the time.

Paul, aged 17.
Paul has just started working in the local sheet metal factory. He is really enjoying work, and has made a lot of friends who are all in their early 20s. They have started to go down to the local playing fields after work to have a game of football. The team intends to join a Sunday league. After playing, they tend to go to the pub for two or three pints of beer. Because of this, Paul is missing his evening meal and making do with nuts and crisps. Most of the people at work smoke, and Paul is wondering whether he should start to smoke. After all, he doesn't want to appear too young, or he won't be included in the team.

Dianne, aged 16.
Dianne has just started to work for her A-levels at the local college. She doesn't know many people, so she is finding it very difficult. She's also noticed that, since leaving school, she has put on weight and is feeling unfit. She used to be in the school netball and tennis teams, but they don't seem to play those games at college. She has decided that she needs to lose some weight, so she is not eating breakfast or lunch.

Michael, aged 14.
Michael is overweight. His parents run a restaurant and he is allowed to eat what he wants. Because his parents are very busy, he doesn't see them very much. He gets bored in the evening, so he watches a lot of videos or plays computer games. People have started to be horrid to him at school, so he keeps telling his mum that he is ill so that he can stay at home.

HOW HEALTHY ARE YOU?
Look at your lifestyle for a week. Keep a diary and write in it:

- what you have eaten every day
- how much exercise you did
- a record of your general mental well-being – were you happy? Sad?
- any stressful incident and what you did about it
- a sleep record – how much sleep you had, how well you slept, how you felt when you woke up.

Looking at the summaries in this chapter, try to examine your lifestyle critically.

Make up some health related targets for yourself.

Good luck!

Index